Financial Management Handbook for Associations and Nonprofits

Financial Management Handbook for Associations and Nonprofits

Craig Stevens
Kate Petrillo
Dawn Brown

American Society of Association Executives
Washington, D.C.

American Society of Association Executives
1575 I Street, NW
Washington, D.C. 20005-1103
Phone: (202) 626-2723; (888) 950-2723 outside the metropolitan Washington, D.C. area
Fax: (202) 408-9634
E-mail: books@asaenet.org

ASAE's core purpose is to advance the value of voluntary associations to society and to support the professionalism of the individuals who lead them.

Susan Robertson, Senior Vice-President, Marketing and Communications
Baron Williams, Director of Book Publishing

This book is available at a special discount when ordered in bulk quantities. For information, contact the ASAE Member Service Center at (202) 371-0940.

A complete catalog of titles is available on the ASAE Web site at www.asaenet.org/bookstore

Library of Congress Cataloging-in-Publication Data

Stevens, Craig, 1959-
  Financial management handbook for associations and nonprofits /
Craig Stevens, Kate Petrillo, Dawn Brown.— 1st ed.
    p. cm.
    Includes index.
    ISBN 0-88034-277-3 (alk. paper)
  1. Associations, institutions, etc.—Accounting—Handbooks, manuals, etc.
  2. Nonprofit organizations—Accounting—Handbooks, manuals, etc. I.
Petrillo, Kate, 1967- II. Brown, Dawn, 1965- III. Title.

  HF5686.A76S74 2004
  657'.98—dc22

                              2003028158

ISBN 0-88034-277-3

Printed in the United States of America.

10 9 8 7 6 5 4 3 2 1

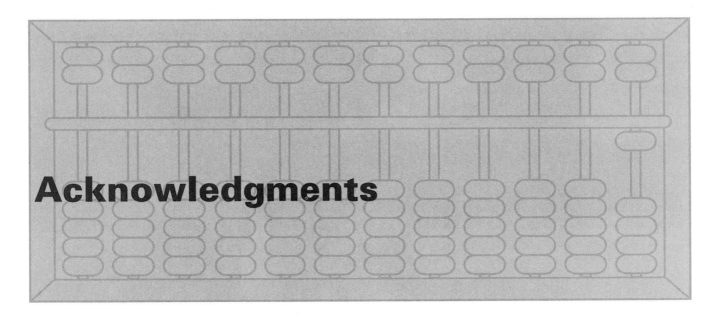

Acknowledgments

This manual was written by the nonprofit team members at Aronson & Company. The primary authors were Kate Petrillo, Dawn Brown, and I. Several other professionals assisted and deserve recognition—thank you to Virginia Geety, Kathy Cuddapah, Michael Yuen, and Ed Burnell for their assistance. Thanks also to Cindy Freer and Dwayne Dixon at Aronson and to Baron Williams. We also want to thank the many clients and colleagues who we have worked with along the way.

Craig Stevens

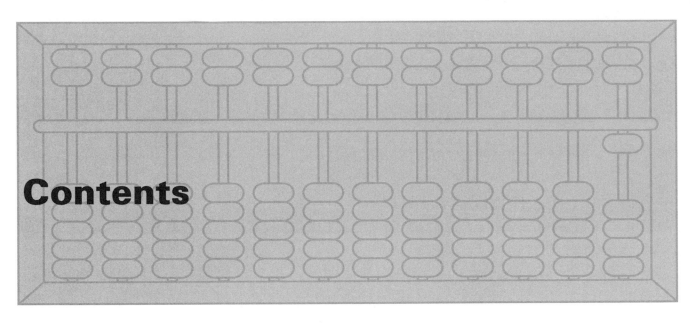

Contents

Chapter 6

Chapter 7

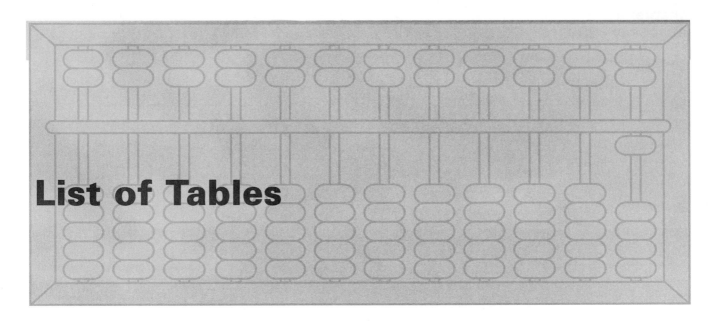

List of Tables

Chapter 4

Chapter 7

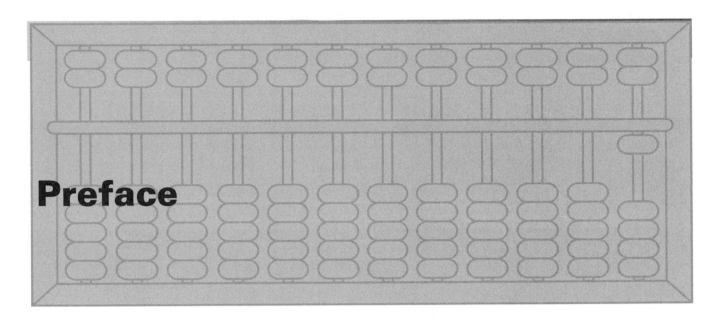

Preface

The world of financial management in associations grows ever more complicated. There is not only the growing number of pronouncements and rules that come into play but the even more challenging aspect of skillfully budgeting and managing an association's finances so they can efficiently carry out their mission and fund the best programs and services for their members.

This manual covers many of the basic areas under the purview of the association financial executive, including an overview of generally accepted accounting principles for associations, recommendations for setting up an accounting system and financial reporting, budgeting, tax matters affecting associations, internal controls, and working with external auditors.

We hope that you find this manual informative and helpful, and we welcome any comments you have to improve future editions.

Craig Stevens
December, 2003

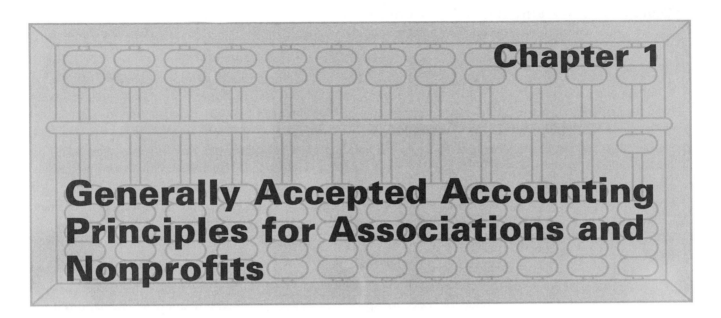

Generally Accepted Accounting Principles for Associations and Nonprofits

This chapter focuses on the sources of generally accepted accounting principles (GAAP) for association and non-profits (collectively "associations") and reviews some of the most typical accounting treatments for associations. Although association personnel have many other duties and generally do not aspire to be experts in GAAP, it is useful to know how to research GAAP questions if they arise.

Defining GAAP

The definition of GAAP is outlined by the American Institute of Certified Public Accountants (AICPA) in their Statement on Auditing Standards No.69 ("The Meaning of Present Fairly in Conformity with Generally Accepted Accounting Principles"). GAAP is defined as consisting of a descending hierarchy of authority consisting of the following:

1. Officially established accounting principles consisting of Financial Accounting Standards Board (FASB) Statements of Financial Accounting Standards and Interpretations, Accounting Principles Board (APB) Opinions, and AICPA Accounting Research Bulletins
2. FASB Technical Bulletins and, if cleared by the FASB, AICPA Industry Audit and Accounting Guides and AICPA Statements of Position
3. AICPA Accounting Standards Executive Committee (ACSEC) practice bulletins that have been cleared by the FASB and consensus positions of the FASB Emerging Issues Task Force
4. AICPA accounting interpretations and implementation guides (Qs & As) published by the FASB staff as well as practices that are widely recognized and prevalent either generally or in the industry

The importance of GAAP is that to receive an unqualified opinion from your independent CPA in a financial statement audit, your financial statements must be in conformity with GAAP. For example, an association can produce its internal monthly financial statements on a cash basis (which is not GAAP), but to receive an unqualified audit opinion, the necessary adjustments must be made to present the audited financial statements on an accrual basis (which is GAAP).

In fact, the FASB statements and other authoritative accounting pronouncements apply only to financial statements meant to be presented in accordance with GAAP. They do not, for example, dictate how an organization keeps its internal financial statements.

Applying Pronouncements to Associations

The basic rule is that all of the various FASB statements, APB opinions, and so forth apply fully to associations, with the following three exceptions:

1. There are certain FASB statements that specifically exempt associations from their application, for example FASB Statement No. 115, "Accounting for Certain Investments in Debt and Equity Securities," specifically exempts associations because they would be covered by FASB Statement No. 124, "Accounting for Certain Investments Held by Not-for-Profit Organizations."

2. Certain financial reporting pronouncements, by the nature of their subject matter, do not apply to associations. For example, APB opinion No. 14, "Accounting for Convertible Debt and Debt Issued with Stock Purchase Warrants," or APB opinion No. 25, "Accounting for Stock Issued to Employees."

3. Certain financial reporting pronouncements are written specifically to specialized industry practices of business enterprises, which would not apply to associations. For example, FASB Statement No. 50, "Financial Reporting in the Record and Music Industry," or FASB Statement No. 65, "Accounting for Certain Mortgage Banking Activities."

However, the pronouncements classified in 2 and 3 above would apply fully to for-profit subsidiaries owned all or in-part by associations. The guidance issued for specialized industries would also apply to associations if they had these types of transactions.

All of the specifics of which pronouncements apply (and how they apply) are contained in the *AICPA Audit and Accounting Guide for Not-for-Profit Organizations,* which is updated annually.[1]

The official pronouncements that apply specifically to associations (which will be covered in this chapter) are the following:

- FASB Statement No. 93, "Recognition of Depreciation by Not-for-Profit Organizations."
- FASB Statement No. 116, "Accounting for Contributions Received and Contributions Made."
- FASB Statement No. 117, "Financial Statements of Not-for-Profit Organizations"
- FASB Statement No. 124, "Accounting for Certain Investments Held by Not-for-Profit Organizations."
- FASB Statement No. 136, "Transfers of Assets to a Not-for-Profit Organization or Charitable Trust That Raises or Holds Contributions for Others."
- AICPA Statement of Position 94-3, "Reporting of Related Entities by Not-for-Profit Organizations."
- AICPA Statement of Position 98-2, "Accounting for the Costs of Activities of Not-for-Profit Organizations and State and Local Governmental Entities that Include Fund-Raising."
- AICPA Statement of Position 98-3, "Audits of States, Local Governments, and Not-for-Profit Organizations Receiving Federal Awards." Keep in mind that FASB and other pronouncements are only applied to material or significant items. They would not apply to insignificant items or transactions.

Basic Accounting Issues for Associations

Aside from the seemingly over-technical area of FASB statements and AICPA Statements of Position, what are some of the common accounting issues facing associations?

Accrual Basis Accounting

One of the basic tenets of GAAP is that financial statements must be presented on the accrual basis of accounting. The accrual basis (distinguished from the cash basis of accounting) means that revenue will be recognized when earned rather than when the cash is received, and expenses will be recognized when incurred, rather than when the cash is paid. This concept applies to associations in numerous ways, such as

---

[1]The AICPA audit and accounting guide for not-for-profit organizations is probably the single most comprehensive guide to accounting issues for associations and non-profits. The guide can be ordered by calling (888) 777-7077.

- Sales of books, publications, CD-ROMs, and other materials
- Receipt of promises to receive contributions
- Costs of producing books, publications, CD-ROMs, and other materials
- Prepayment of expenses such as for insurance, convention-related deposits, security deposits for rent, and so forth
- Purchases of computer equipment and other fixed assets
- Incurrence of expenses before they are paid such as ordering supplies, payroll charges, and so forth
- Receipt of cash for membership dues, conference registrations, and other association services before they are provided
- Receipt of free rent or rent holidays on an office space lease

The accounting treatment of these types of transactions (not meant to be all-inclusive) is described in the sections that follow.

Sale of Books, Publications, CD-ROMS, and Other Materials

Associations often sell these and other types of items to members and nonmembers. Although the trend now is to receive payment by credit card before the item is shipped, other situations will arise where the associations lend credit to the purchaser and ship the item before receiving payment. In this situation, the association would record a receivable for the transaction along with the corresponding revenue represented by the following journal entry:

Accounts receivable[2]	XX	
Publications (other) revenue		XX

When payment is received the cash receipt would be recorded as follows:

Cash	XX	
Accounts receivable		XX

The substance of these entries is that the sales revenue was recorded when earned (when the shipment was made) before the cash was received. This same type of treatment could apply in numerous other situations, such as pledge of contributions (discussed later), seminar or conference attendance before payment, sales of other products and services that were billed, and so forth.

Costs of Producing Books, Publications, CD-ROMS, and Other Materials

In addition to the revenue side of the transaction, there is the matter of recording the cost of producing the books or items sold on the accrual basis. Technically, the full cost of producing the sales item (a book or publication of some kind, for example) would be recorded as inventory as the work is produced.

This could include printing costs, costs of writing the publication if an outside author was paid for the manuscript, or some allocation of staff salaries if the publication was produced internally.[3]

As these costs are incurred they would be recorded as follows:

Inventory	XX	
Cash (accounts payable)		XX

---

[2]Although with most computerized accounting systems, the transaction would be recorded in the general ledger automatically, journal entries will be used throughout this chapter for ease of illustration.

[3]Although correct cost accounting to include a portion of staff salaries and possibly other overhead in the capitalized inventory for the publication, in practice these costs are often expensed as incurred because of the uncertainty of recovering the costs.

Associations would then typically develop a per-unit cost of the publication and, as sales are made, the cost of goods sold would be expensed-out as follows:

Cost of goods sold	XX	
Inventory		XX

The issue of costing out sales of inventory to expense is difficult, because it requires estimates of the ultimate sales volume of the publication or other item, as discussed in the next section.

WRITE-DOWNS   Another important accrual basis concept is the requirement to write down assets to their net realizable value (what will ultimately be collected from their sale, less disposal costs). This concept really applies to all asset categories, including accounts receivable, pledges receivable, investments (discussed later), inventory and fixed assets. Conversely, because of the accounting principle of conservatism, assets are generally never written up to fair value if they increase in value (other than investments, as discussed later). In the inventory context, an assessment must be made at periodic intervals of the ultimate salability of the items, and adjustments are required if the carrying value of the asset exceeds its recovery value. For example, assume Association X has a certain publication that is included in inventory at $10,000 (based on capitalized printing costs and the costs paid to an outside author to write the manuscript). Association X printed 1,000 copies of the publication and planned to cost-out $10 for each unit sold.

$$\frac{\$10,000}{1,000} = \$10 \text{ per sale}$$

By the third year of the publication, however, Association X has sold 500 copies (leaving $5,000 in inventory), and because of changes in the industry it is clear that very few or none of these publications will sell in the future. At year-end, or whenever it becomes clear of the loss in value Association X would then write down the $5,000 as follows:

Inventory Obsolescence Expense (or cost of goods sold)	$5,000	
Inventory		$5,000

This same principle would be applied to the evaluation of the collectibility of accounts receivable (pledges receivable) through a provision for bad debt expense.

Prepayment of Expenses

Another example of accrual accounting is where associations prepay certain expenses prior to their being used up or recognized as expenses. Examples of the kinds of expenditures paid and when they would be considered expenses under accrual accounting would be as shown in Table 1.1.

Some associations take great effort to categorize as assets as many expenditures as possible to improve their bottom line. This is generally not a good practice, and only those expenses that are material and clearly and that have a useful life beyond the balance-sheet date should be shown as prepaid expenses or other assets. All other purchases should be expensed as incurred.

Table 1.1 Expense Recognition under Accrual Accounting

Expenditure	Expense Recognition
Annual insurance premium	Ratably per month over the term of the policy
Conference convention-related deposits and expenditures	Expensed when the conference occurs
Certain major supplies	Expensed over the use of the supplies
Software purchases	Expensed over the useful life of the software
Web site development costs	Discussed later, see discussion in the next section
Rent security deposit	Never—if deposit is returned or upon lease expiration for unreturned portion

Purchases of Computer Equipment and Other Fixed Assets

Associations purchase various fixed assets and intangible assets to assist them in achieving their mission. Examples include

- Office furniture and fixtures
- Computer hardware
- Computer software
- Web site development costs
- Association headquarters building

Generally, those purchases would be charged to expense over the useful life of the asset through depreciation charges. For example, if Association Y purchased $12,000 of computer hardware that was expected to have a useful life of 4 years, the entries would be as follows:

Computer hardware	$12,000	
Cash (accounts payable)		$12,000

To record the purchase of the fixed assets

Depreciation expense	$3,000	
Accumulated depreciation (computer hardware)		$3,000

To record the annual depreciation on hardware purchased

Likewise, computer software costs for purchased software would be expensed over its useful life. The accounting for internally developed software and Web site development costs are subject to special rules described in the next paragraph.

The AICPA issued SOP 98-1, "Accounting for the Costs of Computer Software Developed or Obtained for Internal Use" to provide guidance on when such costs should be capitalized and when they should be expensed. The SOP concluded that costs incurred in the preliminary project stage, such as costs incurred to develop, evaluate, and select alternatives should be expensed immediately. Costs incurred in the application development stage, such as designing the software configuration and interfaces, coding, installation, and testing should be capitalized and amortized over the software's useful life. Costs incurred in the post-implementation and post-operating stages, such as training and maintenance costs, would again be expensed.

In 2002, the Emerging Issues Task Force issued EITF 00-2, "Accounting for Web Site Development Costs." Similar to the approach taken in SOP 98-1, the EITF identified various stages of development and determined the accounting for the costs incurred in each stage. The stages identified by the EITF were the planning stage, the application and infrastructure development stage, the graphics stage, the content development stage, and the operating stage.

Activity in the planning stage generally includes developing a business plan, determining the functions, identifying the hardware and software needs, arranging vendor demonstrations of products available, evaluating alternatives for meeting the entity's needs, and ultimately deciding on the final alternatives. Costs incurred in this stage should be expensed. The application and infrastructure development stage normally involves acquiring or developing the hardware and software to operate the Web site. Costs incurred in this stage should be accounted for in accordance with SOP 98-1, which generally requires capitalization of these costs. Graphics involve the overall design of the Web page, such as the use of borders, colors, fonts, and so forth. Costs incurred in this stage should also be accounted for in accordance with SOP 98-1, which generally would require capitalization except for data conversion costs, which should be expensed. Content would include articles, product photos, maps, charts, and so forth. A conclusion on the accounting for the costs of creating content was not reached by the EITF. The costs of entering the initial content into the Web site should be expensed as data conversion costs. The operating stage normally encompasses training, administration, and maintenance. Cost incurred in this stage should be expensed. However, the costs of significant upgrades or enhancements should be treated as new software if they improve the functionality of the software, and the guidance in SOP 98-1 should be followed.

Association controllers responsible for the accounting for internal use software and Web development costs should ensure that the vendors of the related software and services provide invoices that are detailed enough for the breakdown of costs into those that should be capitalized and those that should be expensed. The organization's accounting system should be reviewed to ensure internal costs incurred on these projects are also captured appropriately.

Although hard assets like office furniture could have a long useful life like 10 years, the trend is to expense computer hardware and software over relatively short useful lives like 3 to 4 years. The technology changes so quickly that these assets become obsolete rapidly. Another current issue is that associations are raising the capitalization threshold to $1,000 or more to avoid the inefficiency of doing a lot of fixed-asset accounting. Some associations purchase office buildings to serve as their headquarters. This asset would generally have a long depreciable life like 30 to 40 years. Land is not a depreciable asset, however, so the portion of the purchase price attributable to the land would not be depreciated. For example, the ABC Association purchased a headquarters building for $1.5 million, of which $300,000 was determined to be the value of the land component of the purchase. The remaining $1.2 million would then be depreciated over the estimated useful life of 30 years in this case, or $40,000 per year.

Incurrence of Expenses before Payment

Many association purchases are done through trade credit and will be paid at a later date. The accrual basis would dictate that these items would be recorded when received rather than when paid. For example, if an association ordered supplies to be paid on credit upon ordering, the entity would record the following information:

Supplies expense	XX	
Accounts payable		XX
To record the purchase of supplies		

Then when the supplies are paid they would record

Accounts payable	XX	
Cash		XX
To record the payment of the item		

Another common example would be the incurrence of payroll costs prior to their payment. This could be the unpaid salaries between pay periods or accrual of a liability for the earned vacation leave for employees. Accrued leave is required to be recorded when earned by employees, and is therefore expensed prior to the use of the actual vacation time (FASB Statement 43).

Receipt of Cash before Providing the Service

A major item on the balance sheet of most associations is deferred revenue. This arises from receiving cash prior to providing the corresponding services and earning the revenue. The most common areas are membership dues, conferences, seminar registrations, and subscriptions to magazines or periodicals on an annual basis.

MEMBERSHIP DUES   Members are the lifeblood of most, if not all, associations. Even if membership dues are a small part of the association budget, the members are still providing the buying power to induce vendors, exhibitors, and others to provide non-dues income.

The basic accounting concept of membership dues is that they should be recognized as revenue as the membership services are provided. In 99% of the cases, this will be ratably over the membership year. For example, if membership dues are $300 per year, for ABC Association and they are paid by Member X on June 15 for the ensuing July 1 through June 30 Membership (and fiscal) year, at June 30 the Association would record $300 in deferred revenue and then would recognize $25 per month of revenue over the fiscal year as represented by the following journal entries:

Cash	$300	
Deferred revenue		$300
To record receipt of membership dues in advance		

Deferred revenue	$25	
Membership dues revenue		$25

To record the monthly portion of membership dues earned

Although this simplistic example is very easy to follow, there can be complexities that require additional analysis. What if Member X had not paid their dues renewal by July, but instead did not pay it until August 15. In this case, if the membership period covered is still July 1 through June 30, then the dues would still be recognized over that period. A catch-up adjustment would be required to recognize additional revenue in August to make up for July.[4]

CONFERENCE AND SEMINAR REGISTRATIONS Similar to membership dues, associations often receive advance payments for conference and seminar registrations. These payments would be recorded as deferred revenue until the conference is held, at which time the revenue would be recognized as follows:

Cash	XX	
Deferred Revenue		XX

To record receipt of conference revenue in advance

Deferred Revenue	XX	
Conference Revenue		XX

To record conference revenue recognition when the event occurs

PERIODICAL SUBSCRIPTIONS The accounting for periodical subscriptions would be similar to the accounting for membership dues with the subscription revenue recognized over the term of the subscription.

Receipt of Free Rent or Rent Holidays on an Office Space Lease

Another frequent situation is one in which an association enters into an office lease that contains a period of free rent or fixed escalations in the rent. The accounting rules (FASB Statement 13) in this situation require that the rent expense be recognized on a straight-line basis over the term of the lease. For example, assume that XYZ Association entered into a 5-year lease, which for ease of illustration, ran from January 1, 2003, through December 31, 2007, and XYZ reported on a calendar year basis. The lease provided for the rents shown in Table 1.2.

Under this fact pattern, the association would recognize rent expense of $120,000 per year and corresponding deferred rent liability in Year 1, which would be reduced to zero over the term of the lease as indicated in Table 1.3.

Table 1.2 Rent Paid over 5 Years

Year 1	$60,000
Year 2	$120,000
Year 3	$130,000
Year 4	$140,000
Year 5	$150,000
Total rent paid	$600,000

---

[4] Many individual member organizations do not record receivables and corresponding deferred revenue for dues renewals because of the uncertainty of any individual member renewing. This could cause a reconciliation difference between your general ledger (where the receivable would not be recorded) and your membership management system where the receivable for the renewing member might be recorded. In practice, certain corporate member organizations who typically have a much small number of members, more predictable renewals (hopefully), and more frequent than annual billing cycles, may record a receivable and revenue for the renewing member before they have paid.

Table 1.3 Recognition of Rent on a Straight-Line Basis

Debit (Credit)	Year 1	Year 2	Year 3	Year 4	Year 5	Total
Rent expense	$120,000	$120,000	$120,000	$120,000	$120,000	$600,000
Deferred rent liability	$(60,000)	—	$10,000	$20,000	$30,000	—
Cash	$(60,000)	$(120,000)	$(130,000)	$(140,000)	$(150,000)	$(600,000)

Operating Leases and Capital Leases

The financial accounting standards over leases can be very complicated and revolve around the issue of how much of the benefits and risks of ownership of the rented property have been transferred to the lessee.

So-called capital leases are situations where, in substance, the risks and benefits of ownership have been transferred to the lessee, and the lease would be accounted for as if the asset were purchased by the lessee.

Operating leases are where the lessee is, in substance, merely renting the property and would be accounted for as a rental.

If a particular lease meets any one of the following classification criteria it is considered a capital lease:

- The lease transfers ownership of the property to the lessee by the end of the lease term.
- The lease contains an option to purchase the leased property at a bargain price.
- The lease term is equal to or greater than 75 percent of the estimated economic life of the leased property.
- The present value of rental and other minimum lease payments equals or exceeds 90 percent of the fair value of the leased property.

The last two criteria are not applicable when the beginning of the lease term falls within the last 25 percent of the total estimated economic life of the leased property.

If none of the criteria listed earlier are met, the lease is accounted for as an operating lease, no asset or liability is recorded, and rental payments are recorded as rental expense in the income statement in a systematic manner.

If one of the capital lease criteria are met, then an asset and a liability would be recorded as if the asset was purchased at an amount equal to the lesser of the present value of the rental payments or the fair value of the leased property. The leased property would be depreciated in a manner consistent with the association's normal depreciation policy (with a few exceptions); the payments of the lease would reduce the liability; and interest would be recorded on the remaining balance of the obligation as if debt had been used to purchase the asset.

As mentioned, this is a technical and complicated area and does not necessarily occur all that frequently in the association context. An accountant once remarked that the lease rules were written to deal with situations where people were renting airplanes and tankers—no one was concerned with rentals of copiers or automobiles.

Contributions

The accounting for nonprofit organizations was changed dramatically by the issuance of FASB Statement No. 116, "Accounting for Contributions Received and Contributions Made." This statement, issued in 1993, was very controversial, and resulted in many nonprofit organizations recognizing contribution income from restricted contributions sooner than when they previously would have recognized them and, along with FASB Statement No. 117, "Financial Statements of Not-For-Profit Organizations," introduced the concept of unrestricted, temporarily restricted, and permanently restricted net assets, replacing the previous "fund balance" terminology. Net assets represent the excess of assets over liabilities or net worth of a nonprofit organization. Although FASB Statement No. 116 has a major impact on the accounting for charities and other Section 501(c)(3) entities, it may have little or no impact on Section 501(c)(6) trade associations who generally do not receive contributions. The standard could have applicability to Section 501(c)(3) association foundations who receive contributions. FASB Statement No. 116 defines a contribution as "an unconditional transfer of cash or other assets to an entity or a settlement of its liabilities in a voluntary nonreciprocal transfer by another entity acting other than as an owner. Other assets include securities, land, buildings, use of facilities or utilities, material and supplies, intangible assets, services, and unconditional promises to give those items in the future." The financial statement definition of a contribution would be analogous to the income tax rules for someone receiving a charitable contribution deduction—namely that there is no quid pro quo for the contribution.

Typical types of contributions and their donors are given in Table 1.4.

The accounting rules distinguish contributions from exchange transactions. Exchange transactions are transfers in which both parties receive goods or services of commensurate value. Therefore, membership dues, payments for an association's publications, materials, and attendance at conferences are exchange transactions, not contributions. As stated earlier, most, if not all, corporate sponsorship payments to an association are exchange transactions, as the corporation receives a marketing benefit for providing the sponsorship. Corporate sponsorships (gifts) to the scholarship fund of the association's educational foundation would be considered contributions, however.

The accounting rules also distinguish between contributions and agency transactions. An agency transaction is one in which a not-for-profit entity is merely acting as an intermediary between the donor and the beneficiary who has been identified by the donor. This transaction is more frequently associated with federated fundraising organizations like United Way or donor-advised funds of charities in certain cases. The nonprofit receiving funds as an agent would merely record an asset and a liability when the cash is received and then reduce the liability to zero when the amount is paid.

Accounting for Contributions

Assuming that the transaction is a contribution and not an exchange transaction or an agency transaction, how should it be recorded?

The AICPA Audit and Accounting Guide provides some indicators useful in distinguishing contributions from exchange transactions and distinguishing between the contribution and exchange portions of membership dues.[5] Further distinction must be made as to whether the contribution has any donor-imposed conditions or

Table 1.4 Types of Donors and Contributions

Type of Donor and Contribution	Comments
Individual donors—current gifts of cash or securities	Generally only contributions to Section 501(c)(3) organizations are deductible. Taxpayers would not receive deductions for contributions made to a Section 501(c)(4) or 501(c)(6) organization.
Individual donors—deferred gifts such as bequests, charitable gift annuities, charitable remainder trusts, and other deferred gifts	Same as above, although typically given to charities, universities, and the like, association foundations are also competing for these types of gifts in some situations.
Private foundations	Typically only given to Section 501(c)(3) entities that will not engage in lobbying with the funds.
Corporate foundations	Typically given to Section 501(c)(3) charities.
Government grants[6]	Although typically given to Section 501(c)(3) entities some Section 501(c)(6) entities also receive grants.
Corporate sponsorships	Typically these are associated with an event such as a convention and are recorded as part of convention revenue.

---

[5]Although typically not applicable to associations, some nonprofit memberships are more of a marketing tool to receive contributions. For example, the local public television station has "memberships" providing different "benefits" based on the amount of your contribution. Often those memberships are partially contributions and partly dues (or exchange) transactions and would be recorded appropriately. For example, a $100 membership might be valued as a $75 contribution and a $25 payment for services. The contribution element would be recorded immediately, and the dues portion would be recognized ratably over the membership year.

[6]In most situations, government grants are not treated as unconditional contributions for financial reporting and are usually recognized as revenue as the costs are incurred on the grant.

donor-imposed restrictions associated with it. A donor-imposed condition is a situation in which the donor specifies a future and uncertain event that must occur before the contribution will be made (or would give the donor cause to ask for return of any amount given if the condition was not met). For example, if Donor X agrees to provide a $20,000 contribution provided that the association foundation raises an additional $100,000 in contributions, that would be a conditional contribution.

A donor-imposed restriction means that the donor makes a contribution but attaches restrictions to the use or timing of the contribution. In simplified terms, there are three types of restrictions:

1. Permanently restricted—Permanently restricted contributions must be maintained by the organization in perpetuity (endowment funds). For example, Donor Y contributes $1,000,000 to the association educational foundation with the stipulation that the $1 million corpus of the gift must be permanently restricted and only the appreciation, income and dividends can be used to fund the activities of the foundation such as scholarships.
2. Temporarily restricted (purpose restricted)—The donor may stipulate that the contribution must be used for a specific purpose, which would create a temporarily restricted contribution. It is considered temporarily restricted because the restriction can be removed or satisfied by actions of the organization. For example, Donor X contributes money to the Section 501(c)(3) association but stipulates that the contribution must be used to support a particular program of the association. This would be a temporarily restricted contribution because it is restricted to a particular purpose, but only temporarily because the restriction will be met and removed when the assets are spent on the specified purpose.
3. Temporarily restricted (time restricted)—These restricted contributions are situations in which the donor has limited the contribution to later periods of time or specified dates. For example, Donor X provides a $300,000 commitment to the educational foundation to be paid $100,000 this year and $100,000 each of the next 2 years. The outlying 2-year amounts would be considered temporarily restricted because of a time restriction.

Contributions that are not conditional and not restricted are considered unrestricted contributions.

Recording Contributions

Contributions can be received as cash, securities, gifts of hard assets (such as food, computer equipment, and also as gifts of services), and also unconditional promises to give these items in the future. Written or oral agreements with donors who promise to give in the future would be recorded as a receivable and revenue even if the promise is not legally enforceable. To record a promise to give there would have to be sufficient verifiable evidence that the donor had made such a promise to the nonprofit organization. This evidence could be a written agreement, a pledge card or oral promises that can be documented. Unconditional gifts of assets or unconditional promises to give would be recorded as contribution income in the period that either the assets or the unconditional promise was received.

Whether the contribution would be recorded as unrestricted, temporarily restricted, or permanently restricted depends on the factors discussed earlier. Consider the examples given in Table 1.5.

The actual accounting rules require pledges that will be received in future years to be discounted to present value. So the actual receivable recorded would be less than $200,000. This discount would then be amortized to revenue over the 2-year period so the entire $200,000 would ultimately be recorded as the contribution revenue.

Cash	$200,000	
Temporarily restricted contribution revenue		$200,000

To record a contribution restricted by a donor for use in a specific program

Other Contribution Issues

There are a number of other issues to consider in the area of accounting for contributions. Conditional promises to give, as discussed earlier, would not be recorded until the condition is met. When the condition or condition(s) are met, the contribution would be recorded.

In the valuation of contributions, contribution revenue should be measured at the fair value of the contribution received. For receipts of cash, it is easy to determine fair value.

Table 1.5 Examples of Contributions Classified by Restriction Type

	Debit	Credit
Cash	$10,000	
Unrestricted contribution revenue		$10,000
To record an unrestricted cash contribution to the annual campaign of		
an association foundation.		
Contribution receivable	$10,000	
Unrestricted contribution revenue		$10,000
To record an unrestricted pledge by a donor to the foundation. When the cash		
is received the receivable would be reduced.		
Cash	$50,000	
Permanently restricted contribution revenue		$50,000
To record a gift of $50,000 to the endowment fund started by the foundation,		
the earnings of which will be used to provide scholarships to students interested in the industry.		
Cash	$100,000	
Contribution receivable	$200,000	
Unrestricted contribution revenue		$100,000
Temporarily restricted contribution revenue		$200,000
To record a gift from a donor for a $300,000 contribution to be received,		
$100,000 this year and then $100,000 per year for the next 2 years. The		
future amounts are temporarily restricted as they are time-restricted.		

As discussed before, pledges of cash donations in the future would be valued at net present value. This would consist of evaluating the pledges received for collectibility providing a bad-debt reserve and then applying a present value discount to the pledges that are expected to be collected. The valuation would be done by using a risk-free discount rate that is appropriate for the expected term of the promise to give (generally the U.S. Treasury Bill rate).

Gifts of other assets, such as real estate, securities, artwork, life insurance policies, free use of office space, and so forth would also be valued at fair value, which could require an appraisal to determine.

There are also some special considerations for how to record split interest gifts, such as charitable gift annuities, charitable remainder trusts, and so forth. The accounting for these types of gifts can be complicated and is really beyond the scope of this work. An entire chapter in the *AICPA Audit and Accounting Guide for Not-for-Profit Organizations* is devoted to accounting for split-interest gifts.

Contributed Services

Contributed services (donated time and work of volunteers) would also be reported as contribution revenue and as a corresponding expense under two situations. The first situation is one in which the contributed services created or enhanced a nonfinancial asset. For example, if certain members of the church volunteered their time and expertise to build out the previously unfinished basement into a reception hall, the value of their services to create the nonfinancial asset would be capitalized along with the materials as part of the asset cost. This situation is unlikely to arise in the association context.

The second situation for which contributed services would be recorded is one in which the following criteria are met:

1. The services would typically need to be purchased by the organization if they had not been provided by contribution.
2. The services required specialized skills and were provided by individuals possessing these skills (such as services provided by accountants, investment advisors, contractors, teachers, electricians, lawyers, doctors, and other professionals and craftspeople). For example, if a medical doctor donates time to a women's shelter to provide prenatal exams and consultations, the value of the doctor's time would be recorded as revenue and expense as follows:

Program expense (medical program)	XX	
Contributed services		XX

Typically, there are no situations for which associations would have to record donated services, but if the situations did arise, they should be recorded.

Financial Statements of Associations

FASB Statement No. 117, "Financial Statements of Not-for-Profit Organizations," was also issued in 1993 and outlines the requirements for how association financial statements should be presented. As discussed earlier, the FASB and other official pronouncements apply only to financial statements meant to be presented in accordance with GAAP. They do not dictate how an association would present their internal monthly statements. However, because most associations are audited, it is a good practice to have the information accumulated so that preparation of the year-end audited financial statements is not difficult.

FASB Statement No. 117 specifies that a complete set of financial statements for an association should include a statement of financial position, a statement of activities, a statement of cash flows, accompanying notes to the financial statements, and, for voluntary health and welfare organizations, a statement of functional expenses.

The requirements of FASB Statement No. 117 are meant to be no more stringent than the requirements for for-profit organizations. Flexibility is permitted with respect to how the financial statements are presented, as long as the required information discussed earlier is included.

The statement of financial position focuses on the association as a whole and reports the amounts of assets, liabilities, and net assets of the organization. Information about the liquidity of the association should be evident from the statement of financial position through either presenting a classified balance sheet (classifying assets and liabilities as either current or noncurrent) or sequencing assets according to their nearness of conversion to cash and liabilities according to the nearness of their maturity and use of cash.

The statement of financial position should also present a total for net assets—net assets in the three different classes (unrestricted, temporarily restricted, and permanently restricted).

Unrestricted net assets are those that are not subject to any donor-imposed restrictions. Because many associations do not have donors per se, it is possible that all of their net assets are unrestricted. Only a restriction placed by a donor is determinative of whether a restriction exists. Self-imposed limitations, such as board-designated reserves or endowments, do not change the character of an asset from unrestricted, although these designations can be noted in the financial statements.

Temporarily restricted net assets result from contributions whose use is limited by donor-imposed stipulations that either expire by the passage of time or are fulfilled and removed by the organization's spending resources on the specified activity requested by the donor. Temporarily restricted net assets often result from multiyear grant pledges from private foundations and contributions to a specific campaign for a particular purpose, such as a building or scholarship fund.

Permanently restricted net assets or endowment funds result from contributions whose use is limited by donor-imposed stipulations that never expire either by the passage of time or actions of the organizations.

A statement of activities should present the revenues, expenses, and changes in net assets of the organization as a whole. The statement should report the amounts of the changes in permanently restricted, temporarily restricted, unrestricted, and total net assets. Some organizations present a separate statement of changes in net assets along with the statement of activities.

Because many associations do not receive contributions, the statement of activities presentation can be very straightforward merely by listing one category of unrestricted revenues and expenses. Complications arise, however, when the organization receives and expends temporarily restricted net assets. The accounting rules stipulate that although temporarily restricted contributions are recorded as temporarily restricted revenues, all expenses are to be reported as decreases in unrestricted net assets. To accommodate this, the use of a line item for net assets released from restrictions is required in the financial statement to balance the decrease in the temporarily restricted net assets. The financial statements presented in Appendix 1.A, "Sample Financial Statements for a Charitable Organization," at the end of this chapter are an example of this transfer.

Another unique element of an association or nonprofit's financial statements is the concept of reporting expenses on a functional basis. A functional basis of expense reporting is where expenses are reported by program or service efforts instead of by natural account classifications. For example, XYZ Association presents their financial statements with the revenue and expense categories given in Table 1.6.

XYZ reports their expenses by program areas, such as member services, conferences, and so forth, instead of by natural classifications, such as salaries, rent, supplies, travel, and so forth.

Table 1.6 Financial Statements Reported on a Functional Basis

Revenue

Membership dues	$XX
Conferences and meeting	XX
Publication sales and advertising	XX
Special assessments	XX
Investment income	XX
Total revenue	XX

Expenses

Member services	$XX
Conferences and meetings	XX
Technical services	XX
Communications, including magazine	XX
Total program expenses	XX
General and administrative	XX
Membership development	XX
Total expenses	XX
Change in net assets	XX

It is a requirement that all nonprofits, including associations, present their expenses by their functional classification, such as major programs and supporting services, either on the face of the statement of activities or in the footnotes to the statements.

A special category of nonprofits, called voluntary health and welfare organizations (generally those organizations whose mission is related to health and welfare issues, and that derive their revenues primarily from voluntary contributions from the general public) is also required to present a special statement called a statement of functional expenses. This statement presents a grid of expenses that shows functional classifications across the top and natural classification down the side, thus presenting expenses in two different ways (see the "Function Expenses" table in Appendix 1.C at the end of this chapter for an example).

Statement of Cash Flows

An association must also present a statement of cash flows providing information about an association's cash receipts and payments during a period; the statement classifies those receipts and payments as resulting from investing, financing, or operating activities. The primary purpose of a statement of cash flows is to provide relevant information about the cash receipts and cash payments of an association during the year. The information included in the statement of cash flows should help members, creditors, and others to assess the association's ability to generate future net cash flows; assess the association's ability to meet its obligations; and assess the reasons for differences between net income and associated cash receipts and payments. The preparation of a cash flows statement can be very technical and is beyond the scope of this work.

Footnotes

Of course, financial statements also must include footnotes that describe in more detail the association's significant accounting policies, and details about other aspects of the association's financial situations. See example financial statements in Appendixes 1.A and 1.B, "Financial Statements for a Sample Association." Most associations utilize their CPA firm to ensure that all of the required footnotes are included; however, there are checklists that can be purchased to identify which disclosures are required.

Comparative Financial Information

Although not required, it is often more useful for associations to present comparative financial statements that show 2 years side-by-side.

Reporting of Related Entities

Another financial reporting consideration is whether related entities to the nonprofit organization should be reporting on a consolidated basis where the financial position and results of activities for related entities would be presented on an aggregated or combined basis.

In 1994, the AICPA issued Statement of Position (SOP) 94-3 to address this topic. SOP 94-3 provides guidance for the following:

- Investments in common stock of majority owned for-profit subsidiaries
- Investment in for-profits, where the nonprofit has a 50% or less voting interest
- Financially interrelated not-for-profit organizations

According to SOP 94-3, nonprofits with a controlling financial interest in a for-profit entity through direct or indirect ownership of a majority voting interest in that entity should generally consolidate unless control is likely to be temporary. For example, a Section 501(c)(6) association has a 100% owned for-profit subsidiary, which conducts certain insurance and other programs. The association would consolidate the for-profit subsidiary in their financial statements. Investment in a for-profit subsidiary in which the association has less than a 50% voting interest would not be consolidated, but it would be on the equity method if the nonprofit had significant influence over the management of the entity. The equity method provides that the investing organization would report their proportionate share of the income or loss of the other entity.

The SOP also describes whether related nonprofit entities should consolidate. For example, if the association creates an education foundation, would those two entities report separately or would they present consolidated statements?

Consolidation of related entities would be required if: one nonprofit has the direct or indirect ability to determine the direction of management and policies of the other organization. Typically this occurs if one entity has the ability to appoint the majority of the board members of the other entity, and they have an economic interest whereby the parent organization is responsible for the liabilities of the other entity, or if the subsidiary organization holds assets that must be used by the parent organization. If both of these criteria are met (control and economic interest), then consolidation is required.

Accounting for Investments

FASB Statement No. 124, "Accounting for Certain Investments Held by Not-for-Profit Organizations" established authoritative guidance for accounting for most stock and bond investments for nonprofits. The guidance provides that investments will be initially recorded at their acquisition cost (including brokerage and other transaction fees) if they were purchased, and recorded at fair value if received as a contribution.

After acquisition, investments in all debt securities and equity securities with readily determinable fair values should be reported at fair value. Debt securities would be investments such as bonds, T-bills, certificates of deposit, and other items that represent debt to the issuer of the investments (such as a bank, government, or corporation).

An equity security has a readily determinable fair value if one of the following three conditions is met:

1. Sales prices are currently available for the security on a Securities and Exchange Commission (SEC) registered exchange, or on the over-the-counter market and such prices are publicly reported by the NASDAQ or by the National Quotations Bureau.
2. If tracked only on a foreign market, that market must be comparable to one of the U.S. markets registered with the SEC.
3. If the security is held in a mutual fund, the fair value per share or unit must be determined, published, and used as the basis for current transactions.

Gains and Losses

The adjustments to fair value will create unrealized gains and losses, which will generally be reported as increases or decreases in unrestricted net assets, unless the appreciation has been restricted (temporarily or permanently) by the donor.

Selling or disposing of investments will create a realized gain or loss. Similar to adjustments to fair value, these gains or losses would be reported as changes in unrestricted net assets unless their use is temporarily or permanently restricted by donor stipulations or by law.

A commonly misunderstood concept is that if securities that have been held for some time are sold, the realized gain or loss reported should exclude the previously recognized unrealized gains and losses. This will result in a different realized gain or loss for financial statement reporting than the actual realized gain or loss on the investment.

For example, suppose that ABC Association purchases some common stocks for $100,000.

Investments	$100,000	
Cash		$100,000

The investments are not subject to any donor stipulations regarding the appreciation or depreciation. In Year 1, the stocks appreciate by $5,000 and also earn $1,000 in dividends that were paid out.

Investments	$5,000	
Cash	$1,000	
Unrealized gain (unrestricted)		$5,000
Dividend income (unrestricted)		$1,000

In Year 2 the stocks depreciated $2,000, and another $1,000 in dividends were paid out.

Cash	$1,000	
Unrealized loss (unrestricted)	$2,000	
Investments		$2,000
Dividend income (unrestricted)		$1,000

At the beginning of Year 3, the stocks were sold for $103,000. Although the total realized gain for the stock from inception was $3,000, the realized gain for the current financial reporting year is zero. This is because, cumulatively, the $3,000 of income had already been recognized.

Investment Income

Investment income includes dividends, interest, rents, royalties, and other similar items; it should be recognized as earned. The income would generally be recognized as unrestricted unless there was a donor stipulation on the use of the income that would restrict its use. For example, Donor X creates an endowment fund stipulating that the corpus of the gift is to be maintained in perpetuity (creating a permanently restricted asset) and that the earnings on the gift are to be used for a particular program. Assume that the association foundation received a $100,000 endowment gift from a donor, and it was invested in bonds.

Investments (bond)	$100,000	
Contributions (permanently restricted)		$100,000

To record the permanently restricted donations and investment in bonds

Subsequently, there was $5,000 in earnings that were restricted by the donor for use in a particular education program.

Cash	$5,000	
Investment earnings (temporarily restricted)		$5,000

To record temporarily restricted earnings

Unrealized Losses

Unrealized losses would also be reported in the statement of activities as decreases in unrestricted net assets, unless they arose from investment assets for which the donor stipulated a restriction on the use of the earnings.

If endowment assets fall below their permanently restricted level, the amount must be made up from unrestricted assets and would be reported as such. The only exception is where prior investment income on the endowment fund was temporarily restricted and had not been used. These amounts would be reduced before unrestricted assets are charged. For example, Donor X created an endowment fund for $100,000 for which the earnings were to be used for a specific program. Cumulatively the earnings not yet expended (but previously recorded) on the specified purpose at a fiscal year-end were $2,000, and the value of the endowment fund dropped to $90,000.

Investment loss (temporarily restricted net assets)	$2,000	
Investment loss (unrestricted net assets)	$8,000	
Investments		$10,000

To record the reduction in investment value as reducing temporarily restricted net assets to the extent unreleased and then reducing unrestricted net assets

If there were no temporarily restricted assets accumulated, then the loss would be shown as a decrease in unrestricted net assets.

Other Investments

Other investments by associations (such as partnerships, real estate, closely held corporations) would be reported at either fair value or at the lower of cost or fair value. The general preference would be to record these items at the lower of cost or fair value. Declines in the value of the investment (which may be difficult to determine) would be recognized as losses, and subsequent recoveries of market value would be recorded with the limitation that the carrying amount would not exceed the original cost.

Although beyond the scope of this work, there are also some specific accounting rules related to investments in derivatives. It is uncommon for associations or other nonprofits to invest in derivatives, however it does happen occasionally when an interest rate swap is done on a headquarters building mortgage.

Expense Recognition Issues

The financial accounting literature distinguishes between revenues and expenses on the one hand and gains and losses on the other. Revenues and expenses represent inflows or outflows from delivering goods, services, or other activities that make up the organization's ongoing major or central activities. Gains or losses represent peripheral or incidental transactions.

For example, a typical association's revenues and expenses would consist of membership dues, conferences and convention revenue, publications, other products and services revenue, and the expenses associated with those functions. Gains and losses would be items such as investment gains and losses, sales of fixed assets not in the ordinary course of business, and insurance recoveries.

As mentioned earlier in the discussion on FASB Statement No. 117, expenses are always reported as decreases in unrestricted net assets. Losses could be reported as decreases in temporarily restricted net assets or, in some cases, as decreases in permanently restricted net assets.

All nonprofits are required to report expenses by function either in the statement of activities or in the notes to the financial statements. Voluntary health and welfare organizations are also required to present statements of functional expenses. No similar requirements exist for losses. With regard to functional reporting, expenses are usually classified as either program services or supporting services. Program services represent the activities that result in goods and services being distributed to beneficiaries, customers, or members that fulfill the purposes or mission for which the organization exists. Supporting services represent management and general, fund-raising, and membership development activities.

Advertising Costs

Advertising costs are distinguished from other costs in that they relate to costs incurred to promote specific products or services. Advertising costs should be expensed as incurred or expensed at the first time the advertising takes place, except for direct-response advertising that results in probable future benefits.

Fund-Raising Activities

The accounting literature states that fund-raising costs should be expensed as incurred even if the activities will benefit a future period. The revenues and expenses of certain special fund-raising events (such as dinners, theater parties) may be reported on a net basis (revenues minus expenses on one line item) provided they are not a significant ongoing activity, in which case they should be reported as revenues and expenses separately.

An entire AICPA SOP has been written related to joint costs of activities that include a fund-raising appeal (AICPA SOP 98-2). This pronouncement is very important to charities that do a tremendous amount of fundraising and would like to classify as much of their costs as possible to program-related expenses. The SOP will not be discussed in detail in this work, but should be reviewed if those kinds of activities are undertaken.

Accounting and Administration of Grants

Many nonprofit organizations and associations receive federal grants as part of their activities. Although federal grants a good source of funding, there are a myriad of rules and regulations that go along with receiving them.

Typically, each grant has enabling legislation that authorized the grant program. Some grant programs also have agency administrative regulations that apply to the program contained in the Code of Federal Regulations. Associations should be familiar with any legislation or regulations that affect their program. In addition, there are three major Office of Management and Budget (OMB) circulars that provide certain regulations affecting federal awards:

- OMB Circular A-110, "Uniform Administrative Requirements for Grants and Agreements with Institutions of Higher Education, Hospitals, and other Non-Profit Organizations."
- OMB Circular A-122, "Cost Principles for Non-Profit Organizations."
- OMB Circular A-133, "Audits of States, Local Governments, and Non-Profit Organizations." All of these are available to review at www.whitehouse.gov/omb/circulars.

In general, grants received by nonprofits or associations will be subject to the provisions of the circulars. Associations or nonprofits should establish financial management systems to meet the federal requirements. Some of the major considerations would include

- Tracking cash received and expenditures incurred on each federal award (this could include an allocation of indirect costs in addition to direct charges).
- Recording interest earned on advances of federal funds. Federal cash advances are supposed to be limited to the minimum amounts needed for the actual immediate cash needs of the association. Advances of federal funds should be held in interest-bearing accounts that have FDIC protection, and interest earnings (less $250 per year for administrative reimbursement) should be returned to the government.
- Tracking all program income from each federal award. Program income represents income generated as a result of the federal award—one example would be registration fees from a federally sponsored conference. Program income is discussed in Paragraph 24 of Circular A-110.
- Separately tracking property purchased with federal money. Circular A-110 Paragraph 34 contains equipment standards.
- Maintaining an adequate internal control system to ensure that funds are used only for the purposes for which the money was received.
- Obtaining adequate fidelity bond coverage to protect the federal government's interests.
- Properly tracking amounts used for costs sharing or matching (Paragraph 23 of Circular A-110); and
- Probably most important of all, properly tracking allowable costs to be charged to the grant. These costs must also be compared to the budget of the grant at regular intervals.

Recipients of federal awards are required to report deviations from the approved budget and program plans and to request prior approval for revisions in certain circumstances. Typically, for nonconstruction awards, prior approval is required when any of the following occur:

- The scope or objective of the project has changed.
- There has been a change in a key person named in the grant application.
- The approved project director or principal investigator has reduced their time devoted to the project by 25% or more, or for 3 months.
- More funding is needed.
- A transfer occurs between indirect and direct cost budgets.
- Costs are included that require prior approval under relevant cost principles.
- Funds earmarked for training allowances are transferred to other categories.
- Work that was planned to be done directly was actually subcontracted.

Typically, grantees with grants over $100,000 can transfer funds among direct-cost categories up to 10% of the approved budget unless specifically restricted by the federal awarding agency.

Allowable Costs

The amount that can be charged against a federal award is the sum of allowable direct and allocable indirect costs less any applicable credits.[7] The government will reimburse the organization for the incurrence of these costs on a federal award subject to the limitations of the grant amount, any cost sharing or matching involved, and limitations imposed by statute or by the award. There is no provision for realizing a "profit" in federal awards,[8] reimbursement is limited to the allowable costs incurred.

Allowable costs must meet the following criteria:

- Costs must be reasonable for the performance of the award and be allocable to the award under the A-122 cost principles.
- Costs must conform to any limitations or exclusions set forth in A-122 or in the award as to the types or amounts of cost items.
- Costs must be consistent with the policies or procedures that apply uniformly to both federally financed and other activities of the organization.
- Costs must be accorded consistent treatment.
- Costs must be determined in accordance with GAAP.
- Costs must not be included as a cost or used to meet cost-sharing or -matching requirements of any other federally financed program in either the current or prior period.
- Costs must be adequately documented.

Reasonable and Allocable Costs

Only reasonable and allocable costs can be charged to a federal award. Generally, to be reasonable, a cost must not exceed the amount that would be incurred by a prudent person under the circumstances prevailing at the time the decision was made to incur the costs. Allocability to a particular cost objective, such as a grant, project, service, or other activity, is determined in accordance with the relative benefits received. A cost is allowable to a government award if it is treated consistently with other costs incurred for the same purpose in like circumstances and if it

- Was incurred specifically for the award (direct costs)
- Benefits both the award and other work and can be distributed in reasonable (allocable direct costs) preparation to the benefits received

---

[7]An applicable credit refers to a refund or reduction of expenditures that offset or reduce expensed items, such as purchase discounts, rebates or allowances, insurance refunds, and so forth.

[8]Some nonprofits enter into contracts with the government (as opposed to grants or cooperative agreements), which could have a provision for profit.

- Is necessary to the overall operation of the organization although a direct relationship to any specific cost objective cannot be shown (indirect costs)

Direct and Indirect Costs

Direct costs are those that can be specifically identified with a particular federal grant or other direct activity of the organization. Indirect costs are those that have been incurred for common or joint objectives and cannot be readily identified with a particular final cost objective. Rent, depreciation, human resources, accounting, and executive office costs would be typical indirect costs.

The distinction of what is a direct or indirect cost must be clearly defined because costs may not be charged to an award as a direct cost if any other cost incurred for the same purpose in like circumstances has been allocated to the award as an indirect cost or vice versa. For example, depreciation on certain computer equipment could not be budgeted and charged to a federal award as a direct cost if all other depreciation charges were treated as an indirect cost and were therefore partially allocated to the award through the indirect rate. Allowing that would result in the federal government bearing an unfair burden of the organization's total cost.

In order to properly apply the A-122 cost principles, every organization needs to establish direct cost objectives and determine what costs are considered direct costs. The costs of activities performed primarily as a service to members, clients, or the general public, when significant and necessary to the organization's mission (and that benefits from the organization's indirect costs, such as rent), must be treated as direct costs whether or not allowable and be allocated an equitable share of indirect costs. Examples of direct cost activities include

- Fund-raising campaigns
- Maintenance of membership rolls, subscriptions, publications, and related functions
- Providing services and information to members, legislative or administrative bodies, or the public
- Promotion, lobbying, and other forms of public relations
- Meetings and conferences except those held to conduct the general administration of the organization
- Maintenance, protection, and investment of special funds not used in the operation of the organization
- Administration of group benefits on behalf of members or clients, including life and hospital insurance, annuity or retirement plans, financial aid, and the like

Unallowable Costs

A-122 outlines certain costs that are specifically unallowable and cannot be charged to federal awards. Some of the most common unallowable costs are as follows:

- Certain advertising costs
- Bad debts
- Key-man life insurance premiums
- Contributions to other organizations
- Fines and penalties
- Fund-raising costs
- Costs of investment counsel
- Certain employee relocation costs
- Entertainment or alcohol charges

Disallowed Costs

Upon audit by federal auditors (the Defense Contract Audit Agency [DCAA] or auditors from other agencies) costs could also be disallowed. Typical areas of disallowed costs are

- Labor costs not properly documented through timesheets and an adequate labor charging system. As described in A-122, organizations must have documented payrolls or personnel activity reports (timesheets)

approved by a responsible official of the organization. The timesheets must reflect an after-the-fact determination of the actual activity of each employee. Budget estimates that reflect amounts determined before the services are performed do not qualify as proper support. The timesheets must also account for the total activity for which employees are compensated. For example, salaried employees working overtime must still account for their total activity. If the normal work week is 40 hours, but an executive worked 50 hours, of which 25 hours were on the grant, they could only charge 50% of their time to the grant not 25/40. All employees are required to complete timesheets if they either charge time directly to federal awards or charge time to an indirect cost category that could ultimately be allocated to a federal award. The only individuals not required to complete timesheets are those individuals whose time is 100% direct. The costs should be charged to nonfederal programs.

- Travel costs—Similar to IRS rules, travel costs can be subject to audit disallowance if they are not properly documented or in compliance with A-122 rules. The rules do not require organizations to use the federal per diem rates. They allow travel costs to be charged on an actual basis, on a per diem, on a mileage basis, or as a combination of the two provided that the method used results in charges consistent with those normally allowed by the organization in its regular operation. Differences in cost between first-class airfare and less expensive classes are specifically unallowable except when accommodations less than first-class are not reasonably available to meet mission requirements.

- Subcontract costs—Subcontractors' charges should be adequately documented as to the selection decision and pricing analysis to meet A-110 procurement standards.

- Undocumented costs—A frequent cost disallowance is for misplaced or lost invoices and cost documentation. It is important to retain adequate documentation for each charge.

- Entertainment costs—Costs of amusement, diversion, social activities, alcohol, and the like are specifically unallowable.

Developing an Indirect Cost Rate

Indirect costs represent those costs incurred for a common or joint objective that cannot be readily identified with particular direct objectives. These costs are generally grouped into a common pool and distributed to activities through a cost allocation process.

An indirect cost rate is a ratio expressed as a percentage of an indirect cost pool and divided by an equitable distribution base. Indirect cost rates are established by agreement between the organizations and their cognizant or oversight agency. The indirect cost proposal provides the basis for the review and negotiation leading to the establishment of an organization's indirect cost rate.

These are several different types of indirect cost rates described in A-122 and several different allocations methods. As you can imagine for a larger organization the indirect cost allocation process can get quite complicated.

Appendix 1.C contains an example of an indirect cost rate structure and how it was calculated.

A-133 Audits

OMB Circular A-133 was issued to establish a uniform system of auditing states, local governments, and not-for-profit organizations that expend federal awards. Circular A-133 requires that any such entity that expends $500,000 or more in a year in federal awards must have a single or program-specific audit conducted for that year.[9] Federal awards as defined by A-133 include federal financial assistance (which can take the form of grants, loans, loan guarantees, property, cooperative agreements, interest subsidies, insurance, food commodities, or direct appropriations) and cost-reimbursement contracts.

A-133 outlines the responsibilities of the entity being audited, federal and pass-through agencies, and the auditor. The entity being audited has the following responsibilities:

---

[9]In June 2003, the OMB increased the A-133 audit threshold from $300,000 to $500,000. This will be effective for fiscal years ending after December 31, 2003.

- Identify all federal awards received and expended by the program;
- Maintain internal control over federal programs;
- Comply with laws, regulations, and provisions of grants or contracts related to the federal program;
- Prepare financial statements and the schedule of expenditures of federal awards;
- Contract for the audit and monitor timely submission of reports; and
- Take corrective action on any audit findings.

The entity being audited must submit a reporting package to the Federal Audit Clearinghouse, along with a data collection form, within the earlier of 30 days from the receipt of the auditor's report or 9 months after the end of the audit period. The reporting package consists of the financial statements and schedule of expenditures of federal awards, a summary schedule of prior audit findings, the auditors' reports, and a corrective action plan for any findings noted therein. The auditors' reports include the following:

- Opinion on the financial statements
- Opinion on the schedule of expenditures of federal awards
- Report on internal control related to financial statements and major programs
- Report on compliance with requirements applicable to each major program and on internal control over compliance in accordance with A-133
- Schedule of findings and questioned costs

The data collection form (Form SF-SAC) summarizes the results of the audit in a format prescribed by the OMB. The form must be certified by a senior level representative of the entity being audited and the auditor. The OMB has simplified the manner in which to comply with the submission by requiring online filing at harvester.census.gov.

Nonfederal Grants

Many organizations also receive grants from nonfederal sources, such as private foundations, states, or corporate foundations. Unlike the federal grants, these grants are not subject to a uniform set of requirements. Proper accounting would be determined by the budgets submitted to the funds in your grant proposal and whatever stipulations were contained in the agreement signed. In theory, the cost allocations and budgeting could be almost identical between public or private funders, provided that private funders would accept your labor rates and the indirect costs you propose. Difficulties could arise if the private funder put a limit on your indirect cost rate recovery. For example, ABC Association proposed to a receive a private foundation grant intended to cover the direct costs of the funded project, but limiting indirect costs to 10% of the direct costs. Assume that ABC's approved indirect cost rate for federal purposes is 35%. In this situation, ABC would either agree to cost share and fund the remaining 25% indirect expenses from other sources of revenue, or they would write the proposal showing direct expense line-items for rent, overhead salaries, depreciation, and so forth, which would normally be tracked as indirect expenses. If the second option was approved, ABC would need to reduce their indirect cost pool for federal reporting for the expenses charged directly to the private foundation grant. This must be done so that the same expenses are not being charged twice, one to the private foundation grant as a direct charge and again to a federal grant through an indirect charge.

Another common issue with private funding is one in which a single project is funded from multiple grants. For example, ABC has a $200,000 project for which they have been successful in getting funding from five different sources for $40,000 each. Because it is impossible to determine exactly what costs were paid from each grant, ABC will have to initially record costs at a project level and then allocate them ratably amongst the different funders for reporting purposes.

Appendix 1.A

Sample Financial Statements for a Charitable Organization

Charitable Organization

Audited Financial Statements

and Other Financial Information

Years Ended September 30, 2002 and 2001

Independent Auditor's Report

Board of Directors
Charitable Organization
Washington, D.C.

We have audited the accompanying statements of financial position of **Charitable Organization** as of September 30, 2002 and 2001, and the related statements of activities and changes in net assets and cash flows for the years then ended. These financial statements are the responsibility of the Organization's management. Our responsibility is to express an opinion on these financial statements based on our audits.

We conducted our audits in accordance with auditing standards generally accepted in the United States of America. Those standards require that we plan and perform the audit to obtain reasonable assurance about whether the financial statements are free of material misstatement. An audit includes examining, on a test basis, evidence supporting the amounts and disclosures in the financial statements. An audit also includes assessing the accounting principles used and significant estimates made by management, as well as evaluating the overall financial statement presentation. We believe that our audits provide a reasonable basis for our opinion.

In our opinion, the financial statements referred to above present fairly, in all material respects, the financial position of **Charitable Organization** as of September 30, 2002 and 2001, and the changes in its net assets and its cash flows for the years then ended in conformity with accounting principles generally accepted in the United States of America.

Rockville, Maryland
November 18, 2002

1. Organization and significant accounting policies	**Organization:** Charitable Organization (the Organization), the nation's largest recreation organization with 100,000 members and donors, is dedicated to connecting people and communities by creating a nationwide network of public recreation areas. Founded in 1985, the Organization is located in Washington, D.C., and has field offices in California, Florida, Indiana, Ohio, Pennsylvania, and Massachusetts.

Basis of presentation: Net assets, revenues, and expenses are classified based on the existence or absence of donor-imposed restrictions. Accordingly, net assets and changes therein are classified and reported as follows:

Unrestricted net assets: Net assets that are not subject to donor-imposed stipulations.

Temporarily restricted net assets: Net assets subject to donor-imposed stipulations that will be met in the future either by actions of the Organization (undertaking of project activities) and/or the passage of time.

Permanently restricted net assets: Net assets subject to donor imposed stipulations that they be maintained permanently by the Organization. Generally the donors of these assets permit the Organization to use all or part of the income earned on related investments for general or specific purposes.

When a donor restriction expires, that is, when a stipulated time restriction ends or purpose restriction is accomplished, temporarily restricted net assets are reclassified to unrestricted net assets and reported in the statement of activities as net assets released from restriction. Donor temporarily restricted contributions whose restrictions are met in the same accounting period in which the contribution was originally pledged are reported as unrestricted support.

Revenue recognition: The Organization recognizes all unconditional contributed support in the period in which the commitment is made.

The Organization recognizes membership dues over the membership period.

Amounts received under contracts are recorded as support when the Organization has incurred expenditures in compliance with the purposes for which the contracts were awarded.

Meeting and event registration revenue is recognized in the year the meeting or event takes place.

The Organization receives various types of in-kind support, including contributed professional services. These services are recognized if the services received create or enhance long-lived assets or require specialized skills, are provided by individuals possessing those skills, and would typically need to be purchased if not donated. The amounts recognized as in-kind support are offset by like amounts recognized as expenses. Approximately $225,000 and $22,000 of professional service was donated in 2002 and 2001, respectively, primarily

1. Organization and significant accounting policies (continued)

consisting of legal services provided in cases affecting the Organization's interests (see Note 8, "Legal matters").

The Organization records donated investments, land and property, and equipment at their estimated fair value on the date received.

Other income consists primarily of merchandise and publication sales and rental income from subleased office space. Sales are recorded when the inventory is shipped. Rental income is recorded in accordance with the lease terms.

Cash and cash equivalents: The Organization considers all highly liquid investments with original maturities of 3 months or less to be cash equivalents. The Organization maintains cash balances that may exceed federally insured limits. Management does not believe that this results in any significant credit risk.

Receivables: Receivables contracts represent amounts due for expenses incurred prior to year end under contract terms.

Receivables pledges and grants consist of amounts pledged from various grantors. All pledges are expected to be fully collected.

Other receivables consist primarily of amounts due for event registrations, for sponsorships, and from sublessees for occupancy expenses paid by the Organization on their behalf.

Inventory: Inventory consists of publications and is recorded at the lower of cost (first-in, first-out method) or market value.

Investments: Investments consist of various mutual funds, money market funds, corporate bonds, common stocks, and U.S. Treasury Securities. These investments are reported at fair value based on quoted market prices.

Land: Land consists primarily of property to be used in recreational land development and is valued at the lesser of acquisition cost or estimated net realizable value.

Property and equipment: Property and equipment are recorded at cost and are being depreciated or amortized on a straight-line basis over their estimated useful lives of 3 to 5 years.

Income taxes: The Organization qualifies as a tax-exempt organization under Section 501(c)(3) of the Internal Revenue Code and is classified as a publicly supported organization under Section 509(a)(1) of the Internal Revenue Code. Consequently, no provision for income taxes is reflected in the accompanying financial statements.

Functional allocation of expenses: The costs of the various programs and other activities have been summarized on a functional basis in the statement of activities and changes in

1. Organization and significant accounting policies (continued)

net assets. Accordingly, certain costs have been allocated among the programs and supporting services benefited.

Accounting estimates: The preparation of financial statements in conformity with generally accepted accounting principles requires management to make estimates and assumptions that affect the reported amounts of assets and liabilities and the disclosure of contingent assets and liabilities at the date of the financial statements and that affect the reported amounts of revenues and expenses during the reporting period. Actual results could differ from those estimates.

Reclassification: Certain 2001 amounts have been reclassified to conform to the 2002 presentation.

2. Investments

The Organization's investments are stated at market value and consisted of the following at September 30, 2002 and 2001:

	2002	2001
Money market funds	$167,852	$ 40,599
Fixed-income funds	200,966	213,749
Equity funds	72,961	43,944
Common stock	172,820	322,776
U.S. Treasury securities	28,418	46,702
Corporate bonds	191,218	185,529
Total	834,235	853,299
Less: permanently restricted	(629,078)	(629,078)
Unrestricted investments	**$205,157**	**$224,221**

A portion of this portfolio is considered permanently restricted (see Note 10, "Permanently restricted net assets") and is therefore classified as noncurrent on the accompanying statements of financial position.

Investment income for the years ended September 30, 2002 and 2001 consisted of the following:

	2002	2001
Interest and dividends	$32,829	$51,175
Net realized and unrealized losses	(67,716)	(149,966)
Total	(34,887)	(98,791)
Less: nonoperating portion	(79,431)	(166,157)
Total from operations	**$44,544**	**$67,366**

Management considers all earnings (losses) on temporarily restricted and board-designated investments to be nonoperating. For the permanently restricted investments, Management recognizes earnings equal to the spending rate (5% of the endowments' prior-year market value) as unrestricted revenue from operations. Any remaining earnings or losses after recognition of the spending rate are considered nonoperating.

Sample Charitable Organization
Notes to Financial Statements

3. Receivables—pledges and grants

Receivables—pledges and grants represent the discounted present value of unconditional promises to give made by donors. Management believes all pledges receivable to be fully collectible, and expects them to be realized as follows:

Year Ending September 30	2002	2001
2002	$ —	$ 284,755
2003	189,643	100,000
Total	189,643	384,755
Less: unamortized discount	—	(10,790)
Total	189,643	373,965
Less: current portion	(189,643)	(284,755)
Noncurrent portion	$ —	$ 89,210

4. Deferred support and revenue

Deferred support and revenue at September 30, 2002 and 2001 consisted of the following:

	2002	2001
Advance royalties	$31,758	$ 91,715
Other	6,100	20,000
Total	$37,858	$111,715

On August 3, 1998, the Organization entered into an affinity agreement with a commercial bank. Under the terms of this agreement, the bank will offer consumer credit products and related services to the Organization's members. In return, the Organization will receive royalties based on the number of accounts opened or renewed and the volume of purchase transactions. The bank guaranteed certain minimum earnings to the Organization over the initial 5-year term of the agreement. The Organization is recognizing royalty revenue on a straight-line basis over the 5-year term of the agreement.

5. Commitments under operating leases

The Organization is obligated under noncancelable operating leases for office space in Washington, D.C., and California. The leases expire at various dates through the year 2007. A portion of the California space has been subleased under a 5-year noncancelable agreement. Leases in Florida, Ohio, Indiana, Massachusetts, and Pennsylvania are for terms of less than 1 year, or may be canceled upon written notice to the lessor.

The Washington lease provides for rent adjustments based on increases in real estate taxes and operating expenses as well as increases in the CPI. The lease also provides for one 5-year renewal option. Under the lease, rent for 7 months of the lease term is waived. This waived rent is recognized by an adjustment to rent expense on the straight-line basis over the term of the lease.

In addition, the Organization leases certain equipment under noncancelable operating leases that expire though 2006.

Sample Charitable Organization

Notes to Financial Statements

5. **Commitments under operating leases (continued)**

The following is a schedule by years of future minimum lease payments required under noncancelable operating leases as of September 30, 2002:

Year Ending September 30	Office Space	Equipment	Sublease Rental Income	Total
2003	$157,572	$24,566	$(18,348)	$163,790
2004	54,144	21,596	(18,348)	57,392
2005	54,144	12,576	(18,348)	48,372
2006	54,144	5,615	(18,348)	41,411
2007	13,536	—	(3,336)	10,200
Total future minimum lease payments	$333,540	$64,353	$(76,728)	$321,165

Total rental expense for all operating leases for the years ended September 30, 2002 and 2001 was $367,126 and $309,364, respectively.

6. **Line of credit**

On June 30, 1998, the Organization entered into a revolving line of credit agreement with a commercial bank. Under the agreement, the Organization may borrow up to $300,000. Interest accrues daily at the bank's prime rate, is payable monthly and expires June 30, 2003. No amounts have been advanced under this agreement.

7. **Retirement plan**

The Organization maintains a tax-deferred annuity plan for all employees that is qualified under Section 403(b) of the Internal Revenue Code. Participating employees may make salary reduction contributions to the Plan up to the maximum amount permitted by the Internal Revenue Code. The Organization contributes 6% of each participant's compensation to the Plan, once the participant completes 6 months of service. Retirement expense for the years ended September 30, 2002 and 2001, was $114,673 and $106,854, respectively.

8. **Legal matters**

In the normal course of its operations, the Organization is involved in legal disputes primarily related to claims by individual property owners opposed to the conversion of land to recreational use. Management does not believe the legal matters will have any material impact on the Organization's financial position.

9. **Temporarily restricted net assets**

Activities related to temporarily restricted net assets during the years ended September 30, 2002 and 2001, are as follows:

	Balance at September 30, 2001	Temporarily Restricted Grants and Contributions	Expenditures/ Releases from Restriction	Balance at September 30, 2002
Program A	$ 3,000	$ 70,000	$ 38,000	$ 35,000
Program B	214,210	30,790	131,263	113,737
Program C	22,750	75,000	57,750	40,000
Program D	50,000	—	50,000	—
Program E	121,608	—	—	121,608
Total	$411,568	$175,790	$277,013	$310,345

9. Temporarily restricted net assets (continued)

	Balance at September 30, 2000	Temporarily Restricted Grants and Contributions	Expenditures/ Releases from Restriction	Balance at September 30, 2001
Program A	$50,000	$60,049	$107,049	$ 3,000
Program B	282,816	76,394	145,000	214,210
Program C	90,000	22,750	90,000	22,750
Program D	—	50,000	—	50,000
Program E	127,245	—	5,637	121,608
Total	$550,061	$209,193	$347,686	$411,568

The related assets are classified in the statements of financial position as follows:

	2002	2001
Cash	$ 43,737	$ 50,750
Receivables—pledges and grants, current portion	145,000	150,000
Receivables—pledges and grants, net of current portion	—	89,210
Investments	121,608	121,608
	$310,345	$411,568

10. Permanently restricted net assets

During the year ended September 30, 1997, the Organization established the ABC Endowment Fund. This fund was established from a gift of stock valued at $334,645 at the date of the gift. The donor stipulated that the principal be invested in perpetuity, and a portion of the income earned on the fund may be spent for general operating support for the Organization. The amount spent each year for general support cannot exceed 5% of the fund's market value of the prior year. In 30 years, the Fund will revert to the general endowment policies of the Organization. These policies provide for endowment earnings to be spent at a rate set annually by the board of directors. The current rate is 5% of the endowment's average market value of the prior calendar year.

During the year ended September 30, 1998, the Organization received another endowment gift of $250,000. The donor requested that half of the annual earnings from the endowment be used for general operating expenses and recommended that the other half be used to increase the endowment, with the allowance for the board to override this provision. Therefore, earnings on the endowment are reported as unrestricted revenue. The board follows the general endowment policies described above, and, as such, has permitted only 5% of the fund's prior-year average market value to be spent on general operations. The remaining earnings (losses) are considered a board-designated reserve. This reserve is included in unrestricted net assets in the accompanying financial statements.

At September 30, 2002, the fair value of permanently restricted investments amounted to $489,401, which is $139,577 less than the amount required to be maintained by donor stipulation ($584,645 original gifts plus $44,433 in accumulated investment earnings on the ABC endowment restricted from spending). Management has reclassified $139,577 of

10. **Permanently restricted net assets (continued)**

unrestricted investments to permanently restricted on the 2002 statement of financial position to cover this shortfall.

At September 30, 2001, the fair value of permanently restricted investments amounted to $556,663, which is $72,415 less than the amount required to be maintained by donor stipulation. Management reclassified $72,415 of unrestricted investments to permanently restricted on the 2001 statement of financial position to cover this shortfall.

Appendix 1.B

Financial Statements for a Sample Association

Sample Association

Audited Financial Statements

and Other Financial Information

Years Ended June 30, 20X2 and 20X1

Independent Auditor's Report

Board of Directors
Sample Association
Washington, D.C.

We have audited the accompanying statements of financial position of **Sample Association** as of June 30, 20X2 and 20X1, and the related statements of activities, changes in net assets, and cash flows for the years then ended as well as the statement of functional expenses for the year ended June 30, 20X2. These financial statements are the responsibility of **Sample Association's** management. Our responsibility is to express an opinion on these financial statements based on our audits.

We conducted our audits in accordance with auditing standards generally accepted in the United States of America and the standards applicable to financial audits contained in *Government Auditing Standards,* issued by the Comptroller General of the United States. Those standards require that we plan and perform the audit to obtain reasonable assurance about whether the financial statements are free of material misstatement. An audit includes examining, on a test basis, evidence supporting the amounts and disclosures in the financial statements. An audit also includes assessing the accounting principles used and significant estimates made by management, as well as evaluating the overall financial statement presentation. We believe that our audits provide a reasonable basis for our opinion.

In our opinion, the financial statements referred to above present fairly, in all material respects, the financial position of **Sample Association** as of June 30, 20X2 and 20X1, and the changes in its net assets and its cash flows for the years then ended in conformity with accounting principles generally accepted in the United States of America.

In accordance with *Government Auditing Standards,* we have also issued our report dated August 10, 20X2, on our consideration of **Sample Association's** internal control over financial reporting and on our tests of its compliance with certain provisions of laws, regulations, contracts and grants. That report is an integral part of an audit performed in accordance with *Government Auditing Standards* and should be read in conjunction with this report in considering the results of our audit.

Rockville, Maryland
August 10, 20X2

Sample Association

Notes to Financial Statements

June 30,	20X2	20X1
Assets		
Current assets		
Cash and cash equivalents	$2,155,115	$1,470,695
Accounts receivable	440,359	415,989
Contributions receivable, current portion	25,000	197,666
Prepaid expenses and deposits	48,158	52,852
Total current assets	2,668,632	2,137,202
Investments	1,504,931	1,534,812
Property and equipment, net	150,169	187,456
Contributions receivable, noncurrent portion	—	147,690
Deposits	19,569	19,569
Total assets	$4,343,301	$4,026,729

Statements of Financial Position

	20X2	20X1
Liabilities and Net Assets		
Current liabilities		
Accounts payable and accrued expenses	$1,112,169	$817,003
Refundable advances	564,847	510,551
Deferred membership dues	224,799	130,202
Other deferred revenue	86,238	32,357
Capital lease obligations, current	10,787	9,187
Total current liabilities	1,998,840	1,499,300
Capital lease obligations, noncurrent portion	19,523	30,311
Total liabilities	2,018,363	1,529,611
Net assets		
Unrestricted		
Undesignated	770,199	594,006
Designated	1,348,400	1,534,888
Total unrestricted net assets	2,118,599	2,128,894
Temporarily restricted	206,339	368,224
Total net assets	2,324,938	2,497,118
Total liabilities and net assets	$4,343,301	$4,026,729

Statements of Activities

Years Ended June 30,	20X2	20X1
Changes in unrestricted net assets:		
Revenues:		
Conferences	$2,450,076	$2,309,117
Membership dues	1,914,337	1,835,438
Contributions	517,233	326,766
Federal grants and contracts	977,907	895,385
Products and services sales	890,765	490,972
Nonfederal grants, contracts, and other revenue	222,516	1,118,998
Investment and other income	43,986	160,259
Total	7,016,820	7,136,935
Net assets released from restrictions:		
Satisfaction of program restrictions	117,875	234,517
Total revenues	7,134,695	7,371,452
Expenses:		
Program services:		
Publications	859,812	683,972
Conferences	1,407,184	1,543,624
Federal grants and contracts	977,907	895,385
Nonfederal grants and contracts	232,552	1,185,235
Public affairs	360,190	327,975
Membership services	432,966	254,530
Education and training	396,046	250,805
Other	148,802	160,532
Total program services	4,815,459	5,302,058
Supporting services:		
Administrative expenses	1,580,017	1,404,106
Organizational advancement	437,001	303,503
Governance and committees	312,513	256,427
Total supporting services	2,329,531	1,964,036
Total expenses	7,144,990	7,266,094
Change in unrestricted net assets	(10,295)	105,358
Changes in temporarily restricted net assets:		
Contributions	50,990	326,726
Uncollectible pledges	(95,000)	—
Net assets released from restrictions	(117,875)	(234,517)
Total change in temporarily restricted net assets	(161,885)	92,209
Change in net assets	$(172,180)	$197,567

Statements of Changes in Net Assets

Years Ended June 30	Unrestricted	Temporarily Restricted	Total
Net assets at July 1, 20X0	$ 2,023,536	$ 276,015	$ 2,299,551
Change in net assets	105,358	92,209	197,567
Net assets at June 30, 20X1	2,128,894	368,224	2,497,118
Change in net assets	(10,295)	(161,885)	(172,180)
Net assets at June 30, 20X2	$ 2,118,599	$ 206,339	$ 2,324,938

Statements of Cash Flows

Years Ended June 30,	20X2	20X1
Cash flows from operating activities		
Change in net assets	$(172,180)	$197,567
Adjustments to reconcile change in net assets to net cash provided by operating activities:		
Unrealized losses (gains) on investments	107,338	(4,258)
Depreciation and amortization	57,154	130,461
(Increase) decrease in		
Accounts receivable	(24,370)	98,699
Contributions receivable	320,356	(163,701)
Prepaid expenses and deposits	4,694	35,786
Increase (decrease) in		
Accounts payable and accrued expenses	295,166	23,671
Deferred membership dues	94,597	44,907
Other deferred revenue	53,881	(146,792)
Refundable advances	54,296	(775,683)
Net cash provided (used) by operating activities	790,932	(559,343)
Cash flows from investing activities		
Net investment transactions	(77,457)	(81,228)
Purchase of property and equipment	(19,867)	(5,838)
Net cash used by investing activities	(97,324)	(87,066)
Cash flows from financing activities		
Repayment of obligations under capital leases	(9,188)	(26,289)
Net increase (decrease) in cash	684,420	(672,698)
Cash and cash equivalents, beginning of year	1,470,695	2,143,393
Cash and cash equivalents, end of year	$2,155,115	$1,470,695

Statement of Functional Expenses

Year Ended June 30, 20X2 (with Comparative Totals for 20X1)

	PROGRAM SERVICES					
	Publications	**Conferences**	**Federal Grants and Contracts**	**Nonfederal Grants and Contracts**	**Public Affairs**	**Member Services**
Salaries and benefits	$225,716	$ 307,813	$238,124	$ 14,336	$308,772	$349,770
Purchased services	167,389	127,477	50,508	9,068	12,351	11,582
Occupancy expenses	—	—	—	—	—	—
Meeting expenses	2,597	814,240	276,110	16,757	10,972	26,427
Fulfillment expenses	111,223	2,417	—	—	—	—
Program expenses	—	—	127,605	184,775	—	—
Printing expenses	283,684	58,898	13,035	116	1,999	8,178
Depreciation expense	—	—	—	—	—	—
Postage expenses	47,250	31,945	4,936	760	589	28,757
Communications expenses	1,390	8,000	2,549	357	3,291	3,434
Other expenses	20,563	54,394	5,966	697	22,216	4,818
Allocated indirect costs	—	—	259,074	5,686	—	—
Total 20X2 expenses	**$859,812**	**$1,407,184**	**$977,907**	**$ 232,552**	**$360,190**	**$432,966**
Total 20X1 expenses	$683,972	$1,543,624	$895,385	$1,185,235	$327,975	$254,530

Statement of Functional Expenses

Year Ended June 30, 20X2 (with Comparative Totals for 20X1)

			SUPPORTING SERVICES			
Education and Training	Other	Total Program Services	Administrative	Organizational Advancement	Governance and Committees	Total Support Services
$226,849	$145,307	$1,816,687	$881,971	$328,876	$200	$1,211,047
61,967	250	442,592	97,735	41,873	39,877	179,485
—	—	—	416,671	—	—	416,671
76,604	800	1,224,507	36,589	29,618	240,793	307,000
—	—	113,640	—	—	—	—
—	—	312,380	—	—	—	—
8,829	368	375,107	20,608	15,680	610	36,898
—	—	—	57,154	—	—	57,154
9,601	318	124,156	3,607	14,305	865	18,777
1,760	653	21,434	16,778	2,021	4,033	22,832
10,436	1,106	120,196	313,664	4,628	26,135	344,427
—	—	264,760	(264,760)	—	—	(264,760)
$396,046	$148,802	$4,815,459	$1,580,017	$437,001	$312,513	$2,329,531
$250,805	$160,532	$5,302,058	$1,404,106	$303,503	$256,427	$1,964,036

Statement of Functional Expenses

Year Ended June 30, 20X2 (with Comparative Totals for 20X1)

SUPPORTING SERVICES

	20X2 Total	20X1 Total
Salaries and benefits	$3,027,734	$2,637,713
Purchased services	622,077	400,372
Occupancy expenses	416,671	391,812
Meeting expenses	1,531,507	1,549,420
Fulfillment expenses	113,640	64,082
Program expenses	312,380	1,215,577
Printing expenses	412,005	368,573
Depreciation expense	57,154	129,461
Postage expenses	142,933	129,070
Communications expenses	44,266	43,391
Other expenses	464,623	336,623
Allocated indirect costs	—	—
Total 20X2 expenses	$7,144,990	
Total 20X1 expenses		$7,266,094

1. **Organization and significant accounting policies**

General information: Sample Association (the Association), founded in 1948, is an association of individuals engaged in the field of education. It promotes educational opportunities across all boundaries, serving members and their institutions as well as students and organizations with an interest in education mobility. The Association sets and upholds standards of good practice, provides professional education and training that strengthen institutional programs and services related to education exchange, and advocates for education.

Description of activities:

- *Publications*—The Association produces various publications, magazines, and newsletters. These publications represent the Association's commitment to the ongoing enhancement of educational exchange.

- *Conferences*—The Association provides for various workshops and meetings that serve as a forum for the latest developments in educational exchange. These meetings offer a concentrated opportunity for the exchange of ideas and offer a network for sharing information as it seeks to increase awareness of and support for education.

- *Federal grants and contracts*—Represents expenses related to providing advice and technical assistance, which enhance educational exchange efforts, through the support of the federal government.

- *Nonfederal grants, contracts, and other expenses*—Represents expenses related to providing advice and technical assistance, which enhance educational exchange efforts, through the support of non–U.S. Government enterprises.

- *Public affairs*—Represents expenses incurred to link Association members with Congress and federal agencies, advocating for support for exchange programs, for removing barriers to exchange, and for informing membership of government actions affecting educational exchange.

- *Membership services*—Expenses related to the maintenance of membership information necessary for the provision of member services and the coordination of governance and leadership activities.

- *Education and training*—Expenses for educational activities designed to support professional development by promoting core competencies and communicating timely information critical to successful management of education exchange.

- *Other*—Represents expenses incurred to support program development in an effort to increase education and training programs.

- *Administrative expenses*—Includes the functions necessary to secure proper administrative functioning of the Board of Directors, maintain an adequate working environment, and manage financial and budgetary responsibilities of the Association.

1. Organization and significant accounting policies (continued)

- *Organizational advancement*—Represents expenses incurred to maintain the Association's various fund drives as it seeks to increase awareness of and support for higher education, education in government, and education in the community and to market the Association's products and services.

- *Governance and committees*—Expenses cover all costs relating to the governance structure of the Association. Also included are the costs of various committees of the Association.

Cash and cash equivalents: The Association considers all highly liquid instruments that are to be used for current operations and which have an original maturity of 3 months or less, to be cash and cash equivalents. All other liquid instruments, which are to be used for the long-term purposes of the Association, are classified as investments. The Association maintains cash balances in several financial institutions, which, on occasion, may exceed federally insured limits. The Association does not believe that this represents any significant credit risk.

Accounts receivable: Accounts receivable consists of trade receivables and all amounts are expected to be collected within 1 year.

Contributions receivable (promises to give): Unconditional promises to give that are expected to be collected within 1 year are recorded at net realizable value. Unconditional promises to give that are expected to be collected in future years are recorded at the present value of their estimated future cash flows. The discounts on those amounts are computed using risk-free interest rates applicable to the years in which the promises are received. Amortization of the discounts is included in contribution revenue. The Association expects all promises to give to be realized in total. Conditional promises to give are not included as support until the conditions are substantially met.

Investments: Investments are recorded at fair value as determined by quoted market prices as of the last day of the Association's fiscal year.

Property and equipment: Property and equipment are stated at cost and are depreciated using the straight-line method over their estimated useful lives ranging from 3 to 5 years. Leasehold improvements are amortized over the life of the lease or the estimated useful life of the asset, whichever is less.

The Association capitalizes all purchases above $2,000. When assets are sold or disposed of, the cost and the related accumulated depreciation are removed from the accounts with any gain or loss reflected in operations currently.

Refundable advances: The Association reports nonfederal funds received but not yet expended as refundable advances. The amounts are received on behalf of intended recipients as part of a national awards program. In addition, refundable advances include funds held on behalf of another entity in a bank account in the Association's name.

1. Organization and significant accounting policies (continued)

Deferred membership dues: Payments for membership dues received in advance are recognized as revenue over the membership period. Unamortized dues are reported as deferred membership dues in the statement of financial position.

Other deferred revenue: Payments received in advance that are considered to be for an exchange transaction are deferred to the period in which the transaction takes place.

Unrestricted net assets: Unrestricted net assets consist of undesignated and designated net assets. Undesignated net assets are funds that are currently available to support the Association's operations. Designated net assets consist of unrestricted funds designated by the Association's Board of Directors for a specific purpose. The Association's designated funds are as follows:

- *Fund 1*—Fund 1 comprises funds received from the sale of the previous headquarters facility. Interest earned can be used to pay for rent on the current office space.

- *Fund 2*—This fund comprises contributions and interest earned thereon, from which funds were spent to improve the Association's Headquarters in Washington, D.C., and to retire the Association's mortgage.

- *Fund 3*—Established by the Board of Directors to help the Association become more fiscally independent. The Association placed 20 percent of the Annual Fund contributions into this fund during 1996, in addition to gifts directed specifically towards the fund's purpose.

- *Fund 4*—During 1996, the Association established Fund 4. This Fund supported two primary initiatives: the new Professional Development Program (PDP) and the Reserve Fund.

- *Fund 5*—This fund comprises co-mingled regional funds designated for the support of regional activities.

Temporarily restricted net assets: The Association reports gifts of cash and other assets as restricted support if they are received with donor stipulations that limit the use of the donated assets. When a donor restriction expires, that is, when a stipulated time restriction ends or a purpose restriction is accomplished, temporarily restricted net assets are reclassified to unrestricted net assets and reported in the statement of activities as net assets released from restrictions.

Revenue recognition: Revenue is recognized during the period in which it is earned. Membership dues revenue is recognized over the membership period to which the dues apply. Revenue received in advance and not yet earned is deferred to the applicable period. Revenue from federal grants and contracts is recognized as expenditures are incurred.

Expenses: Expenses are recognized by the Association during the period in which they are incurred. Expenses paid in advance and not yet incurred are deferred to the applicable period.

1. **Organization and significant accounting policies (continued)**

Allocation of expenses: The direct costs of providing various programs and other activities have been summarized on a functional basis. Indirect costs have not been allocated among the programs and supporting services benefited, except to federal grants and contracts activities.

Use of estimates: The preparation of financial statement in conformity with generally accepted accounting principles requires management to make estimates and assumptions that affect the reported amounts of assets and liabilities and disclosure of contingent assets and liabilities at the date of the financial statements and the reported amounts of revenue and expenses during the reporting period. Actual results could differ from those estimates.

Income tax status: The Association has been granted tax-exempt status under Section 501(c)(3) of the Internal Revenue Code. However, the Association is required to report unrelated business income to the Internal Revenue Service and the District of Columbia, as well as pay certain other taxes to local jurisdictions. In addition, the Internal Revenue Service has determined that the Association is not a "private foundation."

2. **Accounts receivable**

Accounts receivable consist of the following:

	20X2	20X1
Federal grants	$310,340	$334,044
Trade receivables	130,019	81,945
Total	$440,359	$415,989

3. **Investments**

Investments consist of the following:

	20X2	20X1
Equity securities	$894,620	$955,607
Fixed income fund	440,781	477,150
Mutual funds	19,983	—
Money market	44,751	—
Government securities	4,267	3,833
Corporate debt securities	100,529	98,222
Total	$1,504,931	$1,534,812

Investment and other income consist of the following:

	20X1	20X1
Unrealized (losses) gains	$(107,338)	$4,258
Interest and dividends	41,603	139,116
Other income	9,722	16,885
Total investment and other income	$43,987	$160,259

4. Property and equipment

A summary of property and equipment at June 30, is as follows:

	20X2	20X1
Leasehold improvements	$86,918	$86,918
Furniture and equipment	54,582	54,582
Computer equipment and software	184,474	164,607
	325,974	306,107
Less: accumulated depreciation and amortization	175,805	118,651
Net property and equipment	$150,169	$187,456

5. Capital lease obligations

The Association was obligated under a capital lease for a copy machine that expired in fiscal year 20X1. In addition, in January 19X9, the Association entered into a 5-year capital lease for a telephone system. Monthly lease payments of $1,118 consist of principal plus interest. The amortization of the leased equipment for the years ended June 30, 20X2 and 20X1, of $10,787 and $14,383, respectively, is included in depreciation and amortization expense. The capital lease agreements are secured by the copy machine and telephone system with a book value of $40,937 and $46,395 at June 30, 20X2 and 20X1, respectively.

The scheduled future minimum lease payments under the capital lease as of June 30, 20X2, for each of the next 5 years and in aggregate, together with the net present value of the minimum lease payments, are as follows:

Year Ending June 30	Amount
20X3	$19,523
20X4	7,566
20X5	6,513
Total future minimum lease payments	33,602
Less: Amount representing interest	3,292
Net present value of future minimum lease payments	$30,310

6. Operating lease

In August 19X9, the Association entered into a 10-year operating lease for office space commencing on January 1, 20X0. The lease requires monthly payments of $19,569 for the first and second lease year and $25,809 for the third through the tenth year. In addition, the lease agreement provides for a prorated share of the operating expenses for the building, including a prorated share of any increase in expenses. Rent expense for 20X2 and 20X1 totaled $414,697 and $390,167, respectively.

Future minimum lease payments under the lease are as follows:

Sample Association

Notes to Financial Statements

6. Operating lease (continued)

Year Ending June 30	Amount
20X3	$309,704
20X4	309,704
20X5	309,704
20X6	309,704
20X7	309,704
Thereafter	774,260
Total	$2,322,780

7. Temporarily restricted net assets

Temporarily restricted net assets are available for the following purposes:

	20X2	20X1
Education exchange programs	$166,277	$326,557
General operations	40,062	41,667
Total	$206,339	$368,224

8. Retirement plan

The Association maintains a defined-contribution retirement plan (the Plan) in accordance with Section 403(b) of the Internal Revenue Code. The Plan covers all employees who meet certain eligibility requirements. During 20X2, the Association voluntarily contributed 5% (up from 3% in 20X1) of each eligible participant's compensation and matched participant salary deferrals up to another 2%. Employer contributions to the plan for 20X2 and 20X1 were $143,987 and $74,235, respectively.

9. Government grants

Revenue from government grants is recognized to the extent of the Association's corresponding expenditures on the basis of allowable direct costs and applied indirect costs at agreed-upon provisional indirect cost rates. The Association has been awarded restricted cooperative agreements from the United States Department of State and various grants from private foundations and other organizations.

10. Commitments and contingencies

The Association has entered into contracts for future annual conferences through 20X4. The contracts are not cancelable without payment of significant lost revenues to the conference site hosts.

11. Related organizations

The Association is related by common exempt activities to its unincorporated chapters, called regions, which operate in various geographic areas around the country. These regions are self-governed, and the Association does not exercise control over their activities. Consequently, the activities of these regions are not included in the financial statements of the Association. The Association and the various regions may enter into routine, but insignificant, transactions throughout the year. Further, the Association has evaluated the risk of potential liabilities that it may be subject to as a result of its relationship with the various regions and believes that its current insurance coverage is adequate to cover such contingencies. There were no amounts due to or from the regions at June 30, 20X2 and 20X1.

Independent Auditor's Report on Other Financial Information

Board of Directors
Sample Association
Washington, D.C.

Our audits were made for the purpose of forming an opinion on the basic financial statements taken as a whole. The other financial information on page 18 is presented for purposes of additional analysis and is not a required part of the basic financial statements. Such information has been subjected to the auditing procedures applied in the audits of the basic financial statements and, in our opinion, is fairly stated in all material respects in relation to the basic financial statements taken as a whole.

Rockville, Maryland
August 10, 20X2

Sample Association

Notes to Financial Statements

June 30, 20X2 and 20X1

Schedule of Unrestricted Assets

Reserve Funds	Undesignated	Fund 1	Fund 2	Fund 3	Fund 4	PDP Fund	Fund 5	Total Designated	Total
Net assets, June 30, 20X0	$433,974	$868,306	$466,801	$63,535	$80,629	$75,257	$35,034	$1,589,562	$2,023,536
Change in net assets	160,032	(85,715)	33,229	4,525	5,798	(5,662)	(6,849)	(54,674)	105,358
Net assets, June 30, 20X1	594,006	782,591	500,030	68,060	86,427	69,595	28,185	1,534,888	2,128,894
Change in net assets	176,193	(191,000)	9,886	1,329	1,702	916	(9,321)	(186,488)	(10,295)
Net assets, June 30, 20X2	$770,199	$591,591	$509,916	$69,389	$88,129	$70,511	$18,864	$1,348,400	$2,118,599

Refer to independent auditor's report on other financial information

Independent Auditor's Report on Compliance and on Internal Control over Financial Reporting, Based on an Audit of Financial Statements Performed in Accordance with *Government Auditing Standards*

Board of Directors
Sample Association
Washington, D.C.

We have audited the financial statements of **Sample Association** as of and for the year ended June 30, 20X2, and have issued our report thereon dated August 10, 20X2. We conducted our audit in accordance with auditing standards generally accepted in the United States of America and the standards applicable to financial audits contained in *Government Auditing Standards,* issued by the Comptroller General of the United States.

Compliance
As part of obtaining reasonable assurance about whether **Sample Association's** financial statements are free of material misstatement, we performed tests of its compliance with certain provisions of laws, regulations, contracts, and grants, noncompliance with which could have a direct and material effect on the determination of financial statement amounts. However, providing an opinion on compliance with those provisions was not an objective of our audit and, accordingly, we do not express such an opinion. The results of our tests disclosed no instances of noncompliance that are required to be reported under *Government Auditing Standards.*

Internal Control over Financial Reporting
In planning and performing our audit, we considered **Sample Association's** internal control over financial reporting in order to determine our auditing procedures for the purpose of expressing our opinion on the financial statements and not to provide assurance on the internal control over financial reporting. Our consideration of the internal control over financial reporting would not necessarily disclose all matters in the internal control over financial reporting that might be material weaknesses. A material weakness is a condition in which the design or operation of one or more of the internal control components does not reduce to a relatively low level the risk that misstatements in amounts that would be material in relation to the financial statements being audited may occur and not be detected within a timely period by employees in the normal course of performing their assigned functions. We noted no matters involving the internal control over financial reporting and its operation that we consider to be material weaknesses.

This report is intended solely for the information of the board of directors, management, and federal awarding agencies and pass-through entities and is not intended to be, and should not be, used by anyone other than these specified parties.

Rockville, Maryland
August 10, 20X2

Independent Auditor's Report on Compliance with Requirements Applicable to Each Major Program and on Internal Control over Compliance in Accordance with OMB Circular A-133

Board of Directors
Sample Association
Washington, D.C.

Compliance
We have audited the compliance of **Sample Association** with the types of compliance requirements described in the *U.S. Office of Management and Budget (OMB) Circular A-133 Compliance Supplement* that are applicable to each of its major federal programs for the year ended June 30, 20X2. **Sample Association's** major federal programs are identified in the summary of auditor's results section of the accompanying schedule of findings and questioned costs. Compliance with the requirements of laws, regulations, contracts, and grants applicable to each of its major federal programs is the responsibility of **Sample Association's** management. Our responsibility is to express an opinion on **Sample Association's** compliance based on our audit.

We conducted our audit of compliance in accordance with auditing standards generally accepted in the United States of America; the standards applicable to financial audits contained in *Government Auditing Standards,* issued by the Comptroller General of the United States; and OMB Circular A-133, *Audits of States, Local Governments, and Non-Profit Organizations.* Those standards and OMB Circular A-133 require that we plan and perform the audit to obtain reasonable assurance about whether noncompliance with the types of compliance requirements referred to above that could have a direct and material effect on a major federal program occurred. An audit includes examining, on a test basis, evidence about **Sample Association's** compliance with those requirements and performing such other procedures as we considered necessary in the circumstances. We believe that our audit provides a reasonable basis for our opinion. Our audit does not provide a legal determination on **Sample Association's** compliance with those requirements.

As described in item X2-1 in the accompanying Schedule of Findings and Questioned Costs, the Association did not comply with a specific requirement that is applicable to a major federal program. Compliance with such requirement is necessary, in our opinion, for the Association to comply with the requirements applicable to that program.

In our opinion, except for the noncompliance described in the preceding paragraph, **Sample Association** complied, in all material respects, with the requirements referred to above that are applicable to each of its major federal programs for the year ended June 30, 20X2.

Internal Control over Compliance
The Management of **Sample Association** is responsible for establishing and maintaining effective internal control over compliance with requirements of laws, regulations, contracts, and grants applicable to federal programs. In planning and performing our audit, we considered **Sample Association's** internal control over compliance with requirements that could have a direct and material effect on a major federal program in order to determine our auditing procedures for the purpose of expressing our opinion on compliance and to test and report on internal control over compliance in accordance with OMB Circular A-133.

Our consideration of the internal control over compliance would not necessarily disclose all matters in the internal control that might be material weaknesses. A material weakness is a condition in which the design or operation of one or more of the internal control components does not reduce to a relatively low level the risk that noncompliance with applicable requirements of laws, regulations, contracts, and grants—that would be material in relation to a major federal program being audited—may occur and not be detected within a timely period by employees in the normal course of performing their assigned functions. We noted no matters involving the internal control over compliance and its operation that we consider to be material weaknesses.

Schedule of Expenditures of Federal Awards
We have audited the basic financial statements of **Sample Association** as of and for the year ended June 30, 20X2, and have issued our report thereon dated August 10, 20X2. Our audit was performed for the purpose of forming an opinion on the basic financial statements taken as a whole. The accompanying Schedule of Expenditures of Federal Awards is presented for purposes of additional analysis as required by OMB Circular A-133 and is not a required part of the basic financial statements. Such information has been subjected to the auditing procedures applied in the audit of the basic financial statements and, in our opinion, is fairly stated, in all material respects, in relation to the basic financial statements taken as a whole.

This report is intended solely for the information and use of the board of directors, management, federal awarding agencies, and pass-through entities and is not intended to be, and should not be, used by anyone other than these specified parties.

Rockville, Maryland
August 10, 20X2

Sample Association

Schedule of Expenditures of Federal Awards

Year Ended June 30, 20X2

Federal Grantor/ Pass-through Grantor/ Program Title	Federal CFDA Number	Federal Expenditures
Major federal awards:		
United States Department of State:		
Educational Program	82.009	$421,925
Training Program for Educational Advisors	19.404	347,849
Educational Program Support	19.420	145,377
Subtotal major federal awards		915,151
Nonmajor federal award:		
United States Department of State:		
Student Assistance Awards Program	N/A	62,756
Total federal awards		$977,907

The accompanying note is an integral part of this shedule

Year Ended June 30, 20X2

NOTE 1—BASIS OF PRESENTATION

The accompanying schedule of expenditures of federal awards includes the federal grant activity of SAMPLE ASSOCIATION and is presented on the accrual basis of accounting. The information in this schedule is presented in accordance with the requirements of OMB Circular A-133, *Audits Of States, Local Governments, and Non-Profit Organizations*. Therefore, some amounts presented in this schedule may differ from amounts presented in the basic financial statements.

Sample Association

Schedule of Findings and Questioned Costs

Year Ended June 30, 20X2

Section I—Summary of Auditor's Results

FINANCIAL STATEMENTS

Type of auditor's report issued: Unqualified

Internal control over financial reporting:

- Material weakness(es) identified? _____ yes __X__ no
- Reportable condition(s) identified that are not considered to be material weaknesses? _____ yes __X__ none reported

Noncompliance material to financial statements noted? _____ yes __X__ no

Federal Awards

Internal control over major programs:

- Material weakness(es) identified? _____ yes __X__ no
- Reportable condition(s) identified that are not considered to be material weakness(es)? _____ yes __X__ none reported

Type of auditor's report issued on compliance for major programs: Qualified

Any audit findings disclosed that are required to be reported in accordance with Section 510(a) of Circular A-133? __X__ yes _____ no

Identification of Major Programs

CFDA Number	Name of Federal Program or Cluster
82.009	Educational Program
19.404	Training Program for Educational Advisors

Dollar threshold used to distinguish between type A and type B programs: $300,000

Auditee qualified as low-risk auditee? __X__ yes _____ no

Year Ended June 30, 20X2

Section II—FINANCIAL STATEMENT FINDINGS

None

Section III—FEDERAL AWARD FINDINGS AND QUESTIONED COSTS

X2-1—REPORTING

Federal Program—Educational Program (CFDA 82.009) and Training Program for Educational Advisors (CFDA 19.404).

Criteria—Grant agreement requires certain timed progress reports and quarterly financial reports.

Condition—The Association is delinquent in submitting the required reports.

Cause—The Association did not have procedures in place to ensure timely filing of required reports.

Recommendation—We recommend that the Association file all of its required reports on time and that procedures be written and implemented to ensure timely filing. To avoid late filing the Association should consider obtaining a written waiver from the granting agency or an extension of time to file.

Management's Response and Corrective Action Plan—Management is aware of the importance of filing timely and accurate reports in connection with the federal grant programs. A restructuring of the department that manages federal grants is underway with plans to hire an Assistant Director of Project Management. One of the major responsibilities of this position will be federal grant reporting and grant administration work.

Sample Indirect Cost Allocation

Sample Organization: Schedule of Functional Expenses
Year Ended September 30, 2001

	Winter Conference	Congress	Membership	Monthly Publication	Directories	Correspondence Courses
Salaries	$225,760	$ 361,431	$138,728	$ 447,279	$ 74,192	$134,478
Fringe benefits	60,540	89,325	34,819	117,949	19,419	39,613
Temporaries	429	7,743	21,060	1,000	165	495
Professional	317,549	486,127	3,801	8,878	31,656	29,894
Advertising and promotion	17,275	26,897	27,948	1,834	2,887	6,080
Bank fees and service charges	—	—	—	—	—	—
Building operating expense	1,480	1,918	2,517	6,031	1,432	1,379
Committees	912	563	10,300	—	—	—
Depreciation	—	—	—	—	—	—
Dues and subscriptions	421	1,421	890	1,231	1,257	266
Education and seminars	—	297	845	1,920	613	807
Equipment	—	—	—	—	—	—
Equipment rentals and leases	—	—	—	545	—	—
Indirect expenses	—	—	—	—	—	—
Insurance	4,237	5,625	17,907	—	—	—
Mailing list rental and purchase	—	—	—	1,400	1,445	4,335
Maintenance	—	—	—	—	—	—
Photocopying	5,425	13,262	4,860	3,282	2,466	3,526
Postage and freight	22,719	36,949	61,572	127,067	13,889	35,704
Printing and typesetting	60,221	79,191	89,960	465,867	13,549	44,492
Publications	—	—	—	—	30,501	47,751
Rent	21,578	29,346	38,517	92,278	21,899	21,112
Royalties	—	—	—	—	—	18,020
Supplies	2,172	2,177	9,849	2,463	1,392	5,128
Telephone	16,958	19,398	16,720	18,852	7,781	7,745
Travel	5,678	4,130	29,497	10,236	1,267	5,539
Total expenses	$763,354	$1,165,800	$509,790	$1,308,112	$225,810	$406,364

Refer to accompanying independent auditor's report on other financial information.

Sample Organization
Schedule of Functional Expenses

	Other Publications	Training	Mailing Lists	Standards and Accreditation	Government Affairs	Grants
Salaries	$310,146	$ 59,655	$55,157	$ 474,192	$35,414	$367,330
Fringe benefits	83,307	17,433	12,836	122,731	9,894	67,392
Temporaries	990	479	—	—	—	15,988
Professional	62,676	21,425	—	414,651	18,031	163,423
Advertising and promotion	13,753	1,278	—	28,441	1,060	938
Bank fees and service charges	—	—	—	—	—	—
Building operating expense	5,022	968	564	4,549	621	680
Committees	—	—	—	174,473	—	—
Depreciation	—	—	—	—	—	—
Dues and subscriptions	672	627	—	966	1,893	639
Education and seminars	896	81	—	2,371	787	—
Equipment	—	175	—	—	—	1,488
Equipment rentals and leases	—	14,067	—	—	—	—
Indirect expenses	—	—	—	—	—	73,193
Insurance	—	—	—	—	—	—
Mailing list rental and purchase	8,670	—	2,721	—	—	—
Maintenance	—	—	—	—	—	—
Photocopying	17,107	9,514	1,126	32,051	1,280	8,142
Postage and freight	36,022	6,409	6,655	30,536	117	6,490
Printing and typesetting	79,068	7,562	4,350	16,484	—	8,191
Publications	—	—	—	—	—	—
Rent	76,988	14,650	8,631	70,074	9,499	16,011
Royalties	44,885	—	—	—	—	—
Supplies	5,247	6,022	187	15,149	198	17,516
Telephone	14,368	7,255	6,449	18,235	3,190	7,723
Travel	12,921	23,407	—	869,703	3,075	229,176
Total expenses	$772,738	$191,007	$98,676	$2,274,606	$85,059	$984,320

Sample Organization

Other Magazine	Program Council	Certification	Online Academy	General and Administrative	Proposal Development	Total
$ 7,991	$ 55,888	$ 9,947	$24,618	$ 723,311	$27,787	$ 3,508,686
2,208	14,284	2,804	6,235	182,467	7,189	884,210
—	—	—	—	17,812	—	66,161
30,000	—	32,725	21,415	269,568	3,500	1,893,904
—	700	1,407	—	36,143	—	166,641
—	—	—	—	101,501	—	101,501
—	171	164	—	3,803	475	31,774
—	719	—	—	53,652	50	240,669
—	—	—	—	143,680	—	143,680
—	110	—	—	30,997	526	41,916
—	—	—	—	4,143	—	12,760
—	—	—	—	36,961	—	38,624
—	113,372	—		—	—	127,984
—	—	—		(73,193)	—	—
—	—	—		35,235	—	63,004
—	—	—		—	—	18,571
—	—	—		29,860	—	29,860
—	1,898	1,015		13,035	103	118,092
7,316	958	1,622		9,514	—	403,539
14,511	55	3,743		20,255	—	907,499
—	—	—		—	—	78,252
—	4,288	2,033		70,103	7,271	504,278
—	—	—		—	—	62,905
—	349	8,163		40,950	538	117,500
—	319	314		15,436	574	161,317
—	9,650	14,410		85,153	1,578	1,305,420
$62,026	$202,761	$78,347		$1,850,386	$49,591	$11,028,747

Sample Organization

Schedule of Determination of Fringe Benefit and Overhead Cost Rates

Year Ended September 30, 2001

Fringe benefit rate

Numerator	
Total fringe benefit costs	$884,210
Denominator	
Total salaries	$3,508,686
Fringe benefit rate	25.20%

Overhead cost rate

Numerator		
Total overhead costs		$1,585,656
Allocated fringe benefit costs applicable to overhead labor ($723,311 × 25.20%)		182,274
Adjusted overhead costs		$1,767,930
Denominator		
Direct labor per statement of functional expenses	$2,757,588	
Allocated fringe benefit costs applicable to direct labor ($2,757,588 × 25.20%)	694,912	
Other direct costs	5,603,435	
Total overhead base		$9,055,935
Overhead cost rate		19.52%

Refer to accompanying independent auditor's report on other financial information.

Sample Organization
Schedule of Fringe Benefit and Overhead Cost Pools

Years Ended September 30, 2001

Schedule of fringe benefit costs

Payroll taxes	$276,647
Health insurance and medical reimbursement	342,176
Pension plan	187,790
Other benefits	77,600
Total fringe benefit costs	**$884,210**

Schedule of overhead costs

Salaries	$723,311
Equipment	36,961
Supplies	40,950
Postage and freight	9,514
Professional	269,568
Travel	85,153
Printing and typesetting	20,255
Rent	70,103
Insurance	35,235
Telephone	15,436
Maintenance	29,860
Building operating expenses	3,803
Photocopying	13,035
Committees	53,652
Depreciation	143,680
Dues and subscriptions	30,997
Education and seminars	4,143
Total overhead costs	**$1,585,656**

Total general and administrative expenses per the statement of functional expenses	**$1,850,386**

Expenses excluded from overhead costs above

Fringe benefits	(182,467)
Temporaries	(17,812)
Advertising and promotion	(36,143)
Bank fees and service charges	(101,501)
Indirect expenses	73,193
Total overhead costs	**$1,585,656**

Refer to accompanying independent Auditor's report on other financial information.

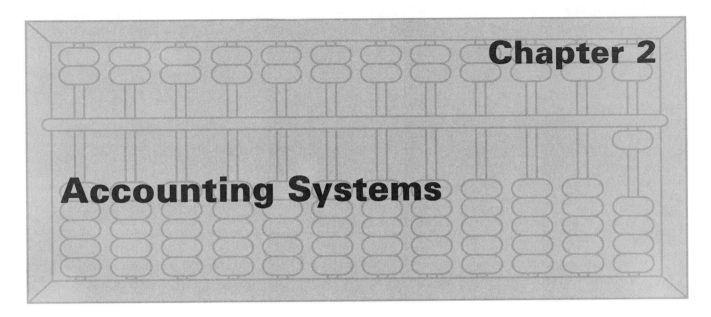

Chapter 2

Accounting Systems

Some of the broad objectives of an accounting and financial management system would include the following:

- Accurate recording of the individual transactions of the association
- Establishing appropriate internal controls to allow the production of financial statements in accordance with GAAP and safeguarding assets from theft and misappropriation
- Accumulating data in a manner to be able to produce accurate and meaningful management reports for internal management, the board of directors, funders, and other constituents
- For organizations receiving federal funding, accumulating the data for reporting to federal agencies
- Accumulating the data needed to produce accurate tax and other information returns. (Form 990, 990-T, and any state or local tax returns necessary, such as real estate, personal property, sales and use tax returns)
- Accumulating data to be able to produce financial statements in accordance with GAAP.

Two of the very important steps in any accounting system are selecting accounting software (discussed in Appendix 2.B, "Overview of Accounting System Selection") and establishing a chart of accounts.

Establishing the Chart of Accounts

The chart of accounts is a comprehensive listing of all the accounts used by an organization and is the foundation on which the general ledger is built. A typical chart is characterized by a numerical arrangement of accounts, with each account having a specific title and corresponding number. Individual transactions are first recorded to the general ledger through the chart of accounts and then grouped and summarized by account to produce reports and financial statements. Although new accounts can be added as they are needed, it is very important to think carefully about the overall structure of the chart because it is time-consuming to change it later.

Because the amounts in the various general ledger accounts will ultimately be rolled up into financial statements, it is important to design the financial statements along with the chart of accounts. There has to be at least one account in the chart of accounts for each line item in each financial statement. Several accounts may be added together for a single line in the statement, but the objective should be to avoid any substantial rearrangement of necessary information.

The particular accounting software will determine the coding sequence for the chart of accounts, but most systems can handle a lengthy, multilevel, numbering system. Some thoughts regarding chart of accounts set-up include

- Determine reporting needs and what you want to record—for instance, when recording travel expenses, what information are you going to need later? Will you want to see subcategories for this expense, such as airfare, meals, and hotel expenses, or are you more interested in the total travel by individual? This information will help determine what subaccounts and structure you might want to include. Also, is there nonfinancial information you want to track? Many accounting systems today include utilities for tracking nonfinancial information, such as head count and square footage to be used in indirect cost allocations.

- Determine what accounts are required to conform with reporting needs (such as GAAP, tax, grant reporting, and so forth)—remember to include categories and accounts that allow you to capture information in accordance with your reporting needs. For instance, keep a separate account for interest and penalties paid rather than lumping these costs in with miscellaneous expenses. This makes preparing an indirect cost allocation plan easier, for instance, because you have isolated unallowable expenses.

- Decide what subaccount structure you need—these decisions flow directly from determining the information you want to record. Here are some things to consider:

  - Do certain departments or divisions need to be grouped together?

  - Do any departments have special projects or programs to be accounted for? Although the general ledger is not the ideal location to do cost accounting, small or limited projects can be successfully tracked with the right account structure.

  - Are any projects to be tracked in the general ledger?

  - What kind of additional breakdowns do you want to see for expenses—an expense by state, by a certain committee, a subtype?

Examples of Account Structures

XXX (Natural Account Number)-XXX (Department)-XXXX (Project)-XX (State)

A food research and promotion association receives dues from its various state chapters. Rather than using separate revenue accounts for each state, the organization uses a single revenue account and a subaccount to designate which state the revenue is from. It uses a job cost system to track all the individual costs by project, but it uses a four-digit project number to reflect the total project cost in the general ledger.

X (Fund Type)-XX (Function)-XX (Department)-XXXX (Natural Account)

An association education foundation has restricted funds, unrestricted funds, and endowment funds. It uses the first segment in its chart of accounts to group funds together by type. This allows for separate balance sheets to be produced for each of the fund groups. Further, an entire function such as general and administrative expenses can be further divided into departments such as finance, office management, and office of the CEO. This allows for easy combination of all the "overhead" departments and still allows for individual department reporting.

XX (Department)-XXXX (Natural Account)-XXX (Customer)

A trade association conducts training and education for its member companies. Each type of training is given its own natural account number. In order to be able to see who took the training, a subaccount is used for each customer. This way the association can determine the total amount of revenue or expense by training type or by customer.

From these examples you can see how a chart of accounts might be structured in order to provide management with the information necessary to run the organization. See Table 2.1 later in this chapter for an example chart of accounts.

Membership or Association Management Systems

Some associations use membership or association management system (AMS) software packages to record membership activity such as dues payments, contributions, event registrations, and so forth.

Backup to an Accounting System

If cash receipts are being processed through your AMS, you must find a way for this information to be input and reconciled to the accounting system. Some AMSs have their own integrated accounting systems. If this system is suitable for the association's needs or can be made so with a little modification, using it may be a good solution. A fully integrated solution is one in which the receipts that are accepted in the membership, events, or convention modules will automatically be updated in both the general ledger and cash management systems. This will, in turn, reflect the activity on the bank statement and provide a clear audit trail.

However, most associations find that for one reason or another the accounting package included with their AMS is not suitable for their needs. In this case, another method of getting the information from or to the AMS is needed.

First, you must determine your flow of receipts. In other words, are the individual departments (for example, the events department) processing the receipts relating to their area, or are the cash receipts being centrally processed through the accounting department?

If the receipts are originating in the functional departments, then the accounting department must verify that the total receipts per batch processed by the other departments match what is being deposited. Batches then would be approved and posted by the accounting department, although the data entry would all be done by the other departments. One of the advantages of this method is that the accounting department is not responsible for applying money to individual customer records, which speeds processing. However, receipts coming into separate departments have a higher probability of being lost, routed incorrectly, or set aside. There is less control of the actual checks or credit card data received.

That is why most association executives would advocate the processing of receipts centrally in the accounting department. In this case the accounting department must separate the receipts into types, create a batch, and log the receipts into the AMS or accounting system. The accounting department would then distribute the receipts to the other functional departments according to the back-up documentation. In this scenario, the information can flow from the accounting system to the AMS, as well as from the AMS, so long as a bridge between the two software programs exists. The disadvantage in this method of receipt processing is the work burden placed on the accounting department. However, the accounting department will maintain more control with this process.

Once you determine what your flow of receipts is, you must then decide which way the data should flow: from the AMS to the accounting system or from the accounting system to the AMS. Most likely, the primary factor in making this decision is going to be the capabilities of the two packages.

One method of integrating the two packages is for one of the systems to create a file that can be imported into the other system either automatically (like upon launching the system) or as some deliberate process. Although the data in both systems may be kept in sync in this manner, there will be a limit to the amount of data that can be transferred. Also, in many cases, transfers from the AMS to the accounting system affect the general ledger only. This means that the cash management system will not be updated with deposit information and will have to be reentered manually if you still want to use the bank reconciliation features of the software. In order to utilize this method, a link or bridge between the two software programs must be created. This can add additional cost to the implementation of the AMS or accounting system. Clearly, however, having some level of integration between the accounting system and the AMS will save a lot of time and is preferred.

Another, more cumbersome method of integrating the two systems is to create a summary entry that can be reentered into the other system. This is a lot more time-consuming and more prone to errors, but can usually be accomplished easily with little monetary investment. The volume of transactions will ultimately dictate the best solution with an automated way of transferring data needed with a higher volume of transactions.

Other integration issues could be present if the association has their receipts processed through a lockbox. With this service (often provided through a bank), the outside provider opens the mail, records payments, processes a deposit, and provides back-up of the transactions for processing through your AMS system. Many association financial executives and outside CPAs strongly advocate the use of a lockbox system to speed up the deposit of funds in the bank and also as an internal control measure. It also is a form of outsourcing (and potential efficiencies) because the association is using bank or lockbox provider personnel to process the receipts.

Cash Receipt Transactions

Types of Receipts

The following sections detail some of the typical types of receipts in a nonprofit organization and the proper way of recording them:

Membership Dues

Membership dues are the periodic amounts collected from individuals or business entities who belong to the organization. In general, dues are for a specified period of time (such as a year) and should be recognized ratably over that time period. For instance if annual dues are $120 per year, then 1/12th, or $10, should be recognized as revenue every month. The dues not yet recognized should be classified as deferred revenue, and an entry should be made each month to relieve the liability account and recognize the appropriate amount as revenue.

Product Sales

As part of their nondues revenue, associations often sell materials related to the mission of their organization, such as books, CDs, and videos. The sale of these items is generally recognized upon shipment as revenue, with a corresponding cost of goods sold entry made.

Conference- and Meeting-Related Receipts

REGISTRATIONS   Registrations are generally any fee collected from an individual for attending a conference or event. Money received prior to the event should be classified as deferred revenue and only recognized as revenue once the event is held.

EXHIBIT FEES   Exhibit fees are paid by companies to display their products to your conference attendees. Like conference registrations, fees paid in advance should be recognized at the time of the conference and deferred prior to the event.

SPONSORSHIPS   Sponsorship fees are paid by business entities to host an event often in connection with a conference. Generally, the fee relates to the cost of the event and would be deferred until the conference is held. Depending on how the sponsorship is structured, income from this activity may be subject to unrelated business income tax (UBIT).

Grants

Nonprofit organizations often receive grants from federal agencies, state agencies, or foundations. Under a grant, typically, the maker of the grant is providing money to cover specific expenses of a project or program. The grant recipient usually must make a report on how these funds were spent and show that they were spent for the expenses specified. Depending on a number of factors, the grant will either be recognized as revenue when it is pledged or received (often as temporarily restricted revenue) or it will be recognized as revenue as the expenses are incurred (typical for a government grant).

Contracts

Contracts are often fixed amounts received for a service performed or product provided. Income is generally recognized as the relevant expenses are incurred or as milestones are reached under the contract.

Forms of Receipts

Direct Receipts

Organizations generally receive at least a portion of their cash receipts directly either by mail or on-site at an event. Wherever possible, a person not responsible for updating AMS records or depositing the cash should open and log all receipts. At an event, receipts should be provided for all transactions and should indicate the method of payment.

CASH   The most difficult receipt to control is cash. When receiving cash, a prenumbered receipt should always be issued to the customer. Then the total cash received should be balanced against the receipt book. If no bank is available for depositing the cash at an event, try posting it as a deposit against your hotel or convention account.

CHECKS   Checks should be restrictively endorsed (i.e., stamped with the name of the organization, the words "For Deposit Only," and the bank account number) and entered into a log. Also, organizations should request that checks be made out with their full name rather than just an acronym. This will prevent potential thieves from creating a fictitious organization with the same acronym and depositing the money.

CREDIT CARDS   Many customers prefer to use credit cards for their transactions. Care must be taken to safeguard the credit card numbers of any customers by tracking who processes the credit card and making sure to securely store or destroy any paperwork that contains credit card information.

Third-Party and Remote Processing

Using a third party to process receipts is a good internal control to safeguard the organization's revenues. There are several types of agencies who provide this service. Although a good deterrent against theft, processing receipts using a third party is more expensive. Each organization must weigh the cost against the potential benefits of such a service.

LOCKBOX   The most common third-party service is a lockbox. This is where the organization rents a box from a bank or other provider. Customers send payments directly to the box, and the bank deposits the payments and sends the back-up to the organization for processing. The main disadvantage of this system is that if the organization segregates or sorts deposit items into separate accounts or for processing similar types of receipts, the bank is very often unable to provide this level of service. The coordination with the bank must be properly planned to achieve your desired results.

FULFILLMENT HOUSE   Fulfillment houses provide the service of filling orders for goods, such as books and CDs, and accepting the payments from the customers. They also provide inventory control and reporting for the organization. Periodically, the organization will receive a check for the proceeds from these sales less the fulfillment house's fees. These vendors provide a useful service for those who do not wish to manage their own inventory.

INTERNET TRANSACTIONS   Many nonprofits have moved into Internet sales for a number of reasons. Primarily, it offers 24-hour access to potential customers. But as an additional feature, customers can purchase products using their credit cards without the risk involved in disclosing their card number. This also alleviates the responsibility on the part of the nonprofit for safeguarding the card information. Credit card processing can take place either through a service that deposits directly to an organization's account or through a host service that makes periodic payments into the organization's account. Associations also generally attempt to create some integration between the internet transactions and their AMS to avoid rekeying the data.

Processing Cash Receipts

Cash receipts should be processed in an expedient manner, meaning that they should be deposited into the bank as quickly as possible. All checks should be restrictively endorsed, and all receipts should be kept in a secure location until they can be deposited in the bank.

For ease of processing, it is suggested that receipts of like type be grouped or batched together. Each batch of items should be given a batch cover sheet, which serves as a control. Entered on this sheet should be the number of items, the total deposit amount, the date, the initials of the individual preparing the batch, and a unique, identifying number. A log of these batches should be maintained so it is possible to identify missing or unposted batches.

A photocopy of the receipt should be made for reference purposes along with a copy of the deposit ticket stamped by the bank. For credit card receipts, many software packages print a daily transaction or transmittal report, which should be run and attached to the receipts.

The batch should then be entered into the accounting system or AMS. Depending on the level of processing that occurs in the accounting department, this could be as simple as creating a batch with the number, date, and amount for later detailed input by another department. It could also mean entering each individual receipt into the system and batching those receipts into deposits for entry. Again, many associations utilize a lockbox service to process their receipt transactions.

Cash Disbursements

Types of Disbursements

There are several types of disbursement or payable transactions: purchases, recurring transactions, conference- and meeting-related expenses, fixed-asset purchases, travel and entertainment expenses, and grant or contract expenses.

Purchases

These are transactions for goods or services that are being ordered, such as office supplies, consulting services, printing services, and the like. Items that recur on a monthly basis but for different amounts, such as telephone charges or other utilities, are generally also included in this category.

Recurring

These are transactions that recur on a periodic basis (monthly, quarterly, etc.) and are for the same amount each period. Some examples of these types of payments are rent, insurance, and note payments.

Conference- and Meeting-Related Expenses

This category of expense includes items or services purchased in conjunction with hosting a meeting event, such as hotel charges, convention center fees, printing of conference materials, conference brochures, and the like. Initially these expenses should be categorized to prepaid expenses and moved to the actual expense category once the event is held.

Fixed-Asset Purchases

A policy should be established by management that establishes what type of items and of what value should be considered fixed assets. A schedule of these items added to fixed assets should be maintained along with the proper documentation for audit purposes.

Travel and Entertainment

Any purchases for food, transportation, hotels, and the like are considered travel expenses. A policy should be established by management that specifies the types and limits on these expenses, what dollar value for which receipts are required (such as all expenses over $25), and what expense items are excluded from reimbursement. In addition, any expense for meals or entertainment should be submitted with the proper IRS documentation, including the dates, the amount, who attended the meeting, and what business matters were discussed.

Grant or Contract Expenses

This includes all direct expenses to the grant or contract as well as any expenses allocated to the grant or contract. Expenses for grants and contracts need to be properly identified and segregated in the general ledger or project management system.

Processing Transactions

One possible scenario for processing transactions would be as follows. All invoices received by the organization should be submitted directly to the accounting department. The accounting department should log these invoices by creating a batch in the accounting system and entering in the invoice information including the account disbursement information if known. This batch should not be posted until the invoices in it are approved. For posting ease, it is often beneficial to separate files according to the approving department to be maintained.

Invoices should then be forwarded to the individual department manager for approval and coding. The manager should then return the invoices to the accounting department. The accounting supervisor can then review the invoices and post the approved batches. This process also allows the accounting department to track and follow-up on invoices that have not been returned by approving managers. Invoice batches should be posted by someone who is not entering the original invoice information. This prevents fake or invalid invoices from being posted. In organizations too small to segregate this duty, the person signing the checks should review the posting journal and invoices when signing to provide this control.

Some organizations use a purchase-order system to process disbursements. This means that when someone wishes to purchase an item or service, they must request a purchase order from the accounting department in advance of placing the order. A purchase-order request with the proper approvals must be completed before the purchase order can be processed. This system provides an additional control by giving the accounting department the opportunity to check whether there are funds available in the budget before a purchase is made. It also speeds disbursement once an invoice is received in that the approvals for the purchase have already been made.

Selection of invoices for payment is based on many things, including available cash, invoice due date, and approval status. Once an invoice has been selected for payment, and the check run, the disbursement journal and checks with the back-up documentation should be reviewed by someone other than the person processing the invoices. When reviewing these items, special attention should be paid to make sure each invoice has the proper approvals.

Payroll

For most associations, their single largest expense is payroll.

Salary Setting

An important part of the payroll process is establishing the correct salary level for each position. In nonprofit organizations it is important that there is a clear connection of the value of the work provided by the individual and the compensation received. Failing to make this correlation could result in *private inurement*—that is, an individual may receive excess benefits from the compensation arrangement, which is prohibited by the IRS.

One of the best methods of determining the correct salary range for a position is to refer to industry salary surveys. Various organizations, including ASAE, produce these surveys on an annual or biannual basis. When using these surveys, special attention should be given to correlate as closely as possible the size, type, and location of the organization because these are primary factors that influence salaries.

Salary Transactions

Salary levels may be recommended by department managers but should ultimately be authorized by the CEO. Authorization to add, terminate, or change a person's salary should be submitted to the accounting department on a payroll change request form and should be signed by one of the authorized individuals. Salary changes for the CEO should be authorized by the board of directors and should be authorized in either the minutes of the organization or with a letter from the president.

Entries into the payroll system should be checked by someone other than the individual entering the payroll prior to posting the transactions or transmitting the payroll to a third-party processor. This person should also review the payroll disbursement journals for inaccuracies or unauthorized transactions. Finally, total disbursement amounts for direct deposits, taxes, and other amounts should be checked on the bank statement to be sure that they match the disbursement journal.

Recording salary expense into the general ledger should be done on the basis of how each individual spends their time (e.g., by project, program, or department). The most accurate method of capturing this information is to use timesheets. Using this method, each accounting unit is charged only for the amount of time each person actually worked. However, in order to save time, some organizations estimate this allocation and then adjust it periodically based on actual time charges for a short period of time.

Other Components of Payroll

In addition to recording the salary expense of payroll, there are a number of other functions that must be performed, including the filing of payroll taxes, payroll tax returns, and other deductions or contributions. There are certain taxes and withholdings that are mandated by the state and federal governments to be withheld from each person's pay. These include social security (FICA), Medicare, federal taxes, and state and local taxes. In the case of social security and Medicare, the employer also makes a contribution matching the amount deducted from the employee. FICA, Medicare, and federal taxes are generally all remitted to the IRS electronically through a system established by the IRS in the last few years. State and local taxes are remitted directly to the state taxing authority generally on a monthly basis. It is important that the tax deposits are made in a timely fashion so as to avoid penalties and interest. Remember, the organization is making these deposits on behalf of the individual. Although the employer is collecting and remitting these payments, it is still the individual's money. At the end of each calendar quarter, a tax return (Form 941) is filed showing all the contributions made and reconciling this against amounts owed.

Voluntary deductions are items that the individual authorizes to be withheld from his or her pay, such as insurance premiums, contributions to the organization's pension plan, contributions to the flexible benefit program, and the like. It is important to remember that these contributions belong to the employee and should be sent to the appropriate plans promptly.

There are certain payroll expenses that the employer must pay beyond what is collected from the employee in the form of mandatory and voluntary contributions. This includes Federal Unemployment Taxes (FUTA), State Unemployment Taxes (SUTA), and Workman's Compensation Insurance. Contributions to FUTA and SUTA are made on a quarterly basis. Workman's Compensation Insurance is generally paid annually.

Many associations outsource the actual processing of payroll checks and remittance of the various payroll taxes to a third-party payroll company. This is often a very efficient way of ensuring that the payroll checks and taxes are handled properly. Many associations involve the use of their human resources (HR) department in parts of the payroll process, especially in salary setting and dispute resolution. Many associations also utilize HR software to assist in the management of the important HR functions.

Investments

Investment Terms

Capital Gains or Losses

When an investment is sold, the amount received above or below cost. For instance, if a bond is purchased for $1,000 and later sold for $950, the capital loss would be $50. If the same bond sold for $1,100, then the capital gain would be $100.

Total Return

The total return is the total amount the investment earns. This amount is calculated by adding dividends, interest income, and capital gains and subtracting capital losses and expenses. For instance, if a bond was purchased for $1,000, earning 10% per year, and sold 1 year later for $950, then the total return would be $50 ($100 interest – $50 capital loss).

Realized Gains or Losses

The realized gain or loss is a gain or loss on an investment recognized when the investment is sold.

Unrealized Gains or Losses

An unrealized gain or loss is an increase or decrease, respectively, in the market value of an investment being held (not sold) as compared to its cost.

Recording Investment Transactions

Each month when the investment statements are received, it is important to analyze them and record all transactions so that the current value of all investments is reported on the financial statements. This process is called *marking to the market,* and it should reflect all changes in the market value of a portfolio including unrealized gains and losses.

However, the process of recording the investment transactions is not as simple as taking the total beginning value of the portfolio, subtracting the ending value, and recording the difference. Each investment within the portfolio must be looked at to determine the amount of interest or dividends received, the amount of the gain or loss of the investment, whether the gain or loss is realized or unrealized, and any interest due on the investment but not yet received. The following is a sample entry:

Investment	15,897	
Interest earned		(5,987)
Unrealized gain on investment		(10,000)
Interest receivable	3,000	
Interest earned	(3,000)	

Notice that interest was accrued that did not increase the value of the investment. This is because on certain investments, such as bonds, interest is only paid periodically. However, interest continues to accrue throughout the term of the investment and must be recorded from month to month.

Investment Policies

Usually the largest assets that a nonprofit owns are its investments. In that regard, most associations create an investment committee of their volunteers who are charged with creating an investment policy, hiring investment managers, and overseeing and monitoring the portfolio operations and results. This committee is typically indemnified through the association's directors and officers insurance. One reason to develop an investment policy is to give guidance on utilizing these assets in a way to meet the organization's cash needs while maximizing investment earnings. Another reason to create an investment policy is to document in a board-approved manner what levels of risk the association is comfortable with, what types of investments are considered appropriate, the performance benchmarks you are shooting for, and what is expected in terms of reporting and monitoring.

Investment policies should contain the following components:

- *Objectives of the portfolio*—The investment objectives of the portfolio should be clearly stated. In other words, is the objective to preserve the corpus of the investment as top priority, are you trying to grow the investments to a certain dollar level, are you trying to generate a certain level of income, or is there some other objective?
- *Target rate of return*—What is the rate you are ideally trying to earn on the portfolio. What is the minimum and maximum levels of return expected for the portfolio? This is usually stated in comparison to a particular industry benchmark, such as the S&P 500 stock index.
- *Acceptable risk*—What is the risk profile of the portfolio? How much fluctuation in the value of your investments is acceptable?
- *Liquidity requirements*—How much cash do you expect to withdraw from the portfolio and at what intervals?
- *Investment horizon*—What is the term of your investments?
- *Asset quality*—What is the minimum acceptable quality rating of investment instruments?
- *Prohibited investments*—What instruments is the investment manager prohibited from buying?
- *Diversification*—How much of any one holding or in any one sector can the portfolio be invested in?
- *Asset allocation*—What is the ideal mix of investments in the portfolio, and what are the minimum and maximum acceptable ranges?

Selecting an Investment Advisor

Many nonprofit organizations decide to seek outside assistance in managing their investment portfolio. There are many reasons for this, but, primarily, outside investment advisors have the resources and expertise to provide in-depth analysis of a portfolio's performance and to help the organization make strategic decisions about their money. The investment manager has the following responsibilities:

- To help the organization in establishing an investment policy and the corresponding asset allocations.
- To help the organization make investment selections within asset groups. Often different managers are employed within each investment sector, such as large-cap domestic equities, domestic bonds, real estate, and foreign equities, because they have specific expertise in that sector.
- To analyze and report on investment performance.

Some individuals would also classify executing the securities transactions and maintaining custody of the assets as functions of the investment manager. In certain cases, this is how these functions are handled. Many organizations select an individual broker from one of the major investment houses as an investment manager. This firm then provides investment advice and executes the trades, and their investment house acts as custodian.

However, an investment manager can be a wholly independent person not affiliated with a brokerage. This person would be compensated on a fee for service basis rather than a transaction basis. A separate firm would then need to be selected whose sole purpose would be to custody the funds and facilitate security transactions. The advantage of this type of relationship is that the investment advisor receives his compensation solely from the fees that are charged and not as commissions or mark-ups on trades. This keeps them wholly independent. However, this type of arrangement could be more expensive than the traditional broker-advisor relationship.

Some organizations will hire a separate investment consultant to advise on establishing an investment policy and hiring mangers for the different asset classes and then to do the reporting and analysis to the investment committee. When selecting an investment advisor, the following list of questions is useful in making a selection:

- What services do you need from the investment advisor?
- How well does the advisor know nonprofits?
- Do you need the advisor's help in establishing an investment policy and asset allocations? How will they do this?
- Will you need someone to execute trades?
- How is the advisor compensated? What is the fee structure?
- What type of reports will the advisor provide and how frequently?
- How will the advisor interact with the investment committee (or other governing body) and how frequently?
- What is the process the advisor uses for selecting portfolio managers (i.e., how is the due diligence performed)?
- What are the benchmarks that will be used in evaluating the accounts?

Reporting

Getting timely and informative reports are the key to understanding the trends and activity in any portfolio. In addition to receiving a report that shows the activity, including unrealized gains and losses on an account, the organization should be receiving regular performance reports. These reports should show how well the portfolio is performing relative to the appropriate indices, how well the portfolio managers are performing relative to others in their peer group, and how the portfolio is meeting the mandates of the investment policy.

Although account statements should be received on a monthly basis, performance reports can be received periodically, such as quarterly or semiannually. However, regardless of how frequently these are reports are received, they need to be reviewed and understood by the governing body. This is crucial so that changes can be made if the portfolio is not meeting expectations.

Inventory

Many nonprofit organizations keep a variety of inventory items from publications to t-shirts. Because this inventory can represent a large investment for the organization, it is important that this asset of the organization be handled prudently.

In-House versus Outsourced Fulfillment

Although many organizations both take and fulfill the orders they receive, many organizations choose to outsource this function to a third party. Fulfillment houses have both the resources and expertise to take and fulfill orders, whereas a nonprofit organization may not. Generally, these houses have storage for the inventory and a sales staff to take and fulfill orders. For a small nonprofit organization with few human resources, this can be a solution.

When selecting a service, it is important that the service will provide information to the nonprofit as well as take and fulfill orders. Fulfillment houses should provide the organization with a monthly report of the inventory sold and current inventory levels. It is important, of course, for the fulfillment house to provide this reporting on a timely basis and in sufficient detail for your needs. This can be helpful in spotting sales trends and identifying slow-moving merchandise. Further, based on their analysis, they should also provide advice on optimum inventory stocking levels.

Generally, outsourcing a noncore function such as this is not more expensive than doing the service in-house. However, special attention should be paid to contract details to ensure that the needs of the organization will be met. One advantage to using a fulfillment house could be their ability to provide sales channels that your association might not have available, such as Web-based catalogs and specialized memberships.

Internal Control

Because inventory is valuable, it is important to have effective internal controls to safeguard it and properly report it on the financial statements. There are many safeguard measures that should be taken to prevent theft or damage, including storing the inventory in a secured area and making sure only authorized individuals have access to this area. Also, requisition forms authorizing withdrawal from inventory should be used. In an automated accounting system, a numbered picking ticket is produced and could be used to track withdrawals from inventory.

An inventory ledger should also be maintained so that a perpetual count of all items is always available. This will help in maintaining inventory levels at the optimum level and with controlling inventory losses. Inventory should also be counted on a periodic basis and the count compared with the inventory ledger. This will help detect any shortages or thefts. Further, if employees know that the inventory is counted, it may prevent future theft of inventory. Procedures should also be established to identify slow-moving inventory for purposes of any necessary write-downs to net realizable value and to determine what controls will be established for the removal of obsolete inventory.

Example Chart of Accounts

As an example of how a chart of accounts might be designed, consider the following sample chart of accounts from a sample trade association developed by the finance and administration section of the American Society of Association Executives (ASAE). Although not presented here, some associations utilize an alphanumeric coding system that could greatly expand your coding possibilities. In this example, the basic accounting numbering system is as follows:

$$XXXX\text{-}XXX\text{-}XX\text{-}XX$$

The first four digits represent the basic account code; the next three digits represent functional codes or programs; the next two digits represent further program codes, if necessary to indicate specific programs or projects; and the final two digits represent the department or division where the activity is conducted.

Basic Account Codes (Four-Digit Account Number)

The four-digit account number is used for the identification of basic accounts and allows for 9,000 possible codes (1000 through 9999). Basic accounts are used to describe the detailed accounts within the balance sheet (statement of financial position) and statement of revenue and expense (statement of activity). The chart of accounts employs the following commonly used structure.

D9.04(1)(a) Financial Administration

1000–3999	Balance sheet accounts
4000–6999	Revenue accounts
7000–9999	Expense accounts

The basic asset, liability, and net asset accounts are grouped by financial statement classifications. The accounts listed within a financial statement grouping will make up that line item total on the financial statements; that is, cash accounts are assigned account numbers 1001 through 1099 and will make up the line item cash on the financial statements. This type of numbering allows the computer to summarize specific accounts into financial statement groupings. These groupings may not be automatic and, accordingly, may need to be coded into the particular software program as the financial statements are being developed.

Remember that accounts may be added to the list as needed, and any that are not needed may be deleted from the list. In this sample, the numbering system allows room for a certain amount of expansion, but if more expansion is needed in particular sections, the optimal numbering structure may differ. The important thing to remember when assigning numbers and account series is to follow a consistent method. The basic accounts can appear within any function or department, but the four-digit number never changes.

The basic revenue and expense accounts are also grouped under financial statement classifications. Various revenue and expense accounts can be combined for financial statement presentation as just described. Basic accounts such as salaries, employee benefits, and rent comprise the natural (i.e., object) classification of expenses.

Each association can add as much detail for each group of accounts as is needed for its particular transactions. Some suggestions of individual accounts are included in parentheses after the general account titles are listed in this illustrative chart of accounts. The following pages contain a basic chart of accounts with a general format of the basic accounts. The suggested revenue and expense accounts is only a guide. Expansion capabilities, which classify amounts by function, program, department, and sample reports, follow the chart of accounts given in Table 2.1.

Each individual receivable account should have an allowance for uncollectible accounts. For example, account 1215 can be used for the allowance for uncollectible dues.

Each net asset (equity) account may have accounts for segregating types of transactions within the equity classification including reclassifications between equity accounts, receipts from donors, or restricted earnings on donor funds. All expenses affect unrestricted equity and may not directly reduce restricted equity accounts; see the Statement of Revenue and Expense given in Table 2.2.

Functional Codes (Three-Digit Account Number Extension)

Basic revenue and expense accounts can be grouped into a financial (i.e., program) statement of revenue and expense. For instance, the expense-line salaries 7050, will most likely appear in every functional area and always have the account number 7050. In establishing a functional classification, some individual expense items may need to be allocated to more than one functional area (i.e., joint costing must be performed). FASB Statement (SFAS) No. 117 requires that the financial statements provide information about expenses reported by their functional classification such as major classes of program services and supporting activities. Under SFAS 117, functional expenses include only the direct expenses related to the function, and general and administrative expenses are a separate function and are not allocated to other functions for purposes of functional reporting. However, for internal reporting purposes, associations may choose to allocate general and administrative expenses (i.e., overhead) to the various program services. Functional coding is accomplished by adding one of the three-digit account codes shown in Table 2.3.

Program Codes (Two-Digit Account Number Extension)

The functional classification of the basic accounts can be expanded by adding a two-digit program (project) code to identify specific programs within a particular functional area. For example, within the functional area

Table 2.1 Basic Chart of Accounts: Balance Sheet

Assets (1000–1999)	**Possible Categories**
Current assets (1000–1599)	
Cash (1000–1099)	
1010 Checking account	Bank A, Bank B, etc.
1020 Imprest accounts	Payroll, etc.
1030 Savings accounts	Bank A, Bank B, etc.
1040 Cash equivalents	Money market, etc.
1050 Cash on hand	Petty cash, etc.
Investments (1100–1199)	
1110 Certificates of deposit	
1120 Mutual funds	
1130 Commercial paper	
1140 Corporate bonds or notes	
1150 Government bonds or notes	
1160 Common stocks	
Receivables (1200–1299)	
1210 Dues	Members, chapters, related organizations, etc.
1220 Products and services	Advertising, exhibitors, registrations, resale, materials, etc.
1230 Contributions and pledges	Members, foundations, corporations, etc.
1240 Grants	Government, foundations, corporations, etc.
1250 Accruals	Interest, etc.
1260 Current portion of long-term receivables	Notes, etc.
Inventories (1300–1399)	
1310 Inventories	Supplies, resale materials, etc.
Prepaid expenses (1400–1499)	
1410 Prepaid expenses	Meetings, trade shows, conventions, insurance, rent, etc.
Other current assets (1500–1599)	
1510 Other current assets	Deposits, advances to employees
Long-term assets (1600–1699)	
Property and equipment (1600–1999)[1]	
1610 Land	
1620 Building	
1630 Building improvements	
1640 Office equipment	
1650 Leased equipment	
1660 Vehicles	

Liabilities (2000–2999)	**Possible Categories**
Current liabilities (2000–2699)	
2010 Accounts payable	
2020 Payroll withholdings	Federal, state, insurance, etc.
2030 Accrued expenses	Rent, retirement, salaries, taxes, vacation, etc.
2110 Notes payable, current	
2210 Mortgage payable, current	
2310 Capital lease obligation, current	
2410 Deferred dues	Members, chapters, related organizations
2510 Deferred revenue	Grants, registration, subscriptions, etc.

[1]Each individual fixed asset should have an accumulated depreciation account. For example, account 1625 can be used for accumulated depreciation of buildings.

Table 2.1   *(continued)*

Liabilities (2000–2999)	Possible Categories

Long-term liabilities (2700–2999)

2710 Notes payable	
2720 Mortgage payable	
2730 Capital lease obligation	
2810 Deferred dues	Amounts received for future fiscal periods
2820 Deferred subscriptions	Amounts received for future fiscal periods
2910 Deferred rent credit	

Net assets (3000–3999)	Possible Categories

Unrestricted (3000–3299)

3010 Undesignated/operating	
3020 Board designated	Contingencies, future programs, building, etc.

Temporarily restricted by donors (3300–3599)

3310 Purpose restricted	Specify purposes
3320 Time restricted	Specify time

Permanently restricted by donors (3600–3999)

3610 Endowment	Specify purpose

Table 2.2   Statement of Revenue and Expense

Revenue (4000–6900)	Possible Categories
4010 Dues	Members, chapters, related organizations, etc.
4110 Initiation fees	
4210 Special assessments	
4510 Registrations	Regular, associate, exhibitor, etc.
4610 Exhibitor fees	
4710 Supplementary activities	Meals, tours, etc.
5100 Advertising	
5200 Subscriptions	
5300 Reprints	
5400 Video and other visual materials	
5500 Royalties	
5550 Certification	
5600 Mailing labels	
5700 Management fees	Related entities, etc.
5800 Administrative fees insurance program, etc.	
5900 Commissions	
6000 Grants	Government, foundation, corporate, and individual
6110 Contributions	Cash, property, services
6210 Services	
6220 Endorsements	
6230 Interest	
6240 Dividends	
6250 Rent	
6260 Gain on sale of investments	
6270 Gain on disposal of operating assets	
6280 Miscellaneous	

Expense (7000–9999)

Table 2.3   Functional Codes for Internal Reporting

Program Code Services	Functional Area
Meetings	100
Education	200
Trade shows	300

Table 2.3 *(continued)*

Program Code Services	Functional Area
Publications	400
Certification	500
Government relations	600
Supporting activities	700
Management and general	800
Fund-raising	900

of publications, there may be a monthly magazine, newsletter, directory, or an education book. In this situation, each publication would be identified with its own two-digit program code. Some examples of specific programs within a functional area are given in Table 2.4.

Department Codes (Two-Digit Account Number Extension)

The next level of expansion in the chart of accounts is by department, division, or responsibility center codes. Departments are usually established based upon staff responsibilities. Individual staff in these departments may have responsibility for particular functional areas and programs. Examples of departments are as given in Table 2.5.

Table 2.4 Program Codes for Internal Reporting

Functional Area	Program	Code
Meetings		100-00
	Annual meeting	100-01
	Regional meetings	100-02
	Board and committee meetings	100-03
Education		200-00
Trade shows	Eastern	300-01
	Western	300-02
	European	300-03
Publications		400-00
	Magazine	400-01
	Newsletter	400-02
	Directory	400-03
	Books	400-04
Certification		500-00
	Testing	500-01
	Renewals	500-02
Government relations		600-00
	Legislative	600-01
	Regulatory	600-02
	Coalitions	600-03
	Issues briefings	600-04

Table 2.5 Department Codes for Internal Reporting

Department	Code
Education	01
Meetings	02
Publications	03
Member relations	04
Administration	05
Government affairs	06

Fund Accounting

Some associations maintain their accounts on a fund basis. SFAS No. 117 states that reporting by fund groups is not a necessary part of external financial reporting. However, SFAS No. 117 does not preclude an association from providing individual assets and related liabilities by fund groups for external or internal financial reporting purposes. Restrictions on assets imposed by donors may be accounted for by maintaining fund basis accounting records. If fund accounting is done, an additional code, possibly at the left of all other codes, can be used to designate funds for asset, liability, equity, and revenue accounts. All expense accounts should have the undesignated net asset (equity) fund code.

Appendix 2.A

Accounting System Documentation

It is very important for an association to have their accounting systems and procedures documented. This documentation serves as a training manual for new staff, improves internal controls by forcing people to think them through and write them down, and is an invaluable document for new CFOs and controllers to learn about the association's accounting requirements and procedures. The accounting manual can either be a formal document or a collection of memos and notes. Both would suffice, provided they cover the essential elements of an organization's accounting policies and internal controls. An example table of contents of a formal accounting manual is as follows:

I. Introduction
II. Accounting Department Overview
    A. Organization
    B. Responsibilities
        1. Job Descriptions
        2. Internal Control and Segregation of Duties
        3. Computer Access and Control
        4. Delegation of Authority
III. General Ledger and Chart of Accounts
    A. Chart of Accounts Overview
        1. Reasons for the Account Structure Used
    B. Control of Chart of Accounts
    C. Procedure for Establishing Accounts
    D. Account Definitions
IV. Budgeting
    A. Overview and Policy
    B. Procedure
        1. Outline of the Steps of the Budgeting Process
        2. Budget Planning
        3. Execution of the Budget Process

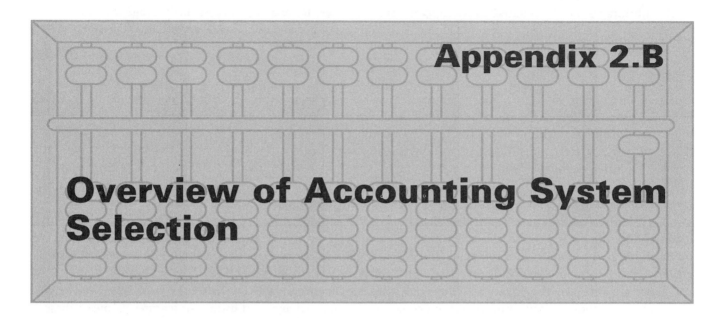

Appendix 2.B

Overview of Accounting System Selection

Selecting an accounting system can be a daunting task: There are many good accounting packages. How is it possible to choose the best for your organization? Selecting a package not suited to your organization can create additional work for the accounting department and frustration among the staff in general. However, selecting an accounting system can be made easier by following a diligent, organized process as outlined in the following sections.

Standard Criteria to Decide on a System

Start by evaluating the organization's needs. This may sound like an unnecessary step, but by clearly defining the organization's needs, it will be easier to identify potential accounting systems. Many organizations have developed functional procedures and processes to take advantage of the features in their current accounting systems. An organization should recognize that it will be necessary to change these procedures and processes in order to take advantage of the new system.

Some general items to consider in selecting a new system would include:

1. What modules are needed—Most accounting systems offer a set of "core" modules, which include general ledger, accounts payable, accounts receivable, payroll, inventory, order entry, job cost, and system manager. In addition to these modules, accounting solutions above the entry level generally offer a host of advanced modules, such as fixed assets, fund and encumbrance accounting, grant accounting, and many others. It is worthwhile to evaluate the current needs of the organization and match module availability. In addition, look at processes that the organization would like to automate in the future and determine whether or not there will be modules to meet these requirements.

2. Character length and segmentation of the account structure—Many organizations need multiple segments and a large number of characters for accounts because of the number of departments, program areas, and projects they perform. Many entry-level systems can be eliminated early on because of an insufficient number of available segments or characters. Equally important in evaluating this feature is whether each segment can be reported separately. In some systems, only one or two primary segments can be used for reporting.

    It should be noted that many systems allow the use of alphanumeric characters in the account structure as opposed to strictly numeric fields. This greatly increases the possible combinations in the chart of accounts. Wherever feasible, organizations should take advantage of this expanded capability.

3. The need for Web modules or a Web-based accounting package—Does the organization have remote users or Web-based sales that necessitate the need for Web modules? Many packages have only limited Web capabilities, which, if needed by the organization (either now or in the future), would make them poor choices. One of

the advantages of a Web-based package is the ability for users to be able to access the package literally anytime, anywhere. However, issues surrounding access by unauthorized users, back-up of data, and hardware maintenance need to be explored thoroughly prior to implementation.

A more comprehensive (but not exhaustive) list of items to consider is included on the General System Questionnaire, shown in Table 2.B.1. When considering these items, it is important to decide what importance they hold. For instance, if an organization sells publications separately and together as a set, the ability to "kit" items might be very important. Conversely, tracking serial number information, although nice, may not be necessary. When looking at systems, it is important to differentiate what is critical to the organization and what is a luxury.

The next step in the selection of an accounting package is to research the available products. This in and of itself can be a daunting task because there are a large number of packages available. Most accounting software manufacturers now have Web sites that provide basic information about their product and the various modules available. Many sites will have online demonstrations and even evaluation tools to help customers choose what modules and features are needed. Another good resource for product information is magazine articles in such publications as *Accounting Technology* or *The Journal of Accountancy*. However, be aware that even magazine articles tend to focus on the positive features of the software and not its weaknesses.

There are also several software selection tools available that are designed to help organizations pick the right software. These tools contain profiles of the various accounting packages and listings of features. Some of these tools are

- The Accounting Library
  1-800-272-4085
  Richmond, VA
  www.excelco.com
  This software will allow the user to select from over 4,000 features needed. The software will then rank the solutions best suited to the customer's needs.
- The Requirements Analyst, CTS, Inc.
  131 Rollins Ave., S-1
  Rockville, MD 20852
  1-800-433-5015
  www.ctsguides.com
  This software helps the user assess needs against mid-level packages.
- Accounting Software Advisor
  www.accountingsoftwarenews.com
  This tool is an interactive guide to current software packages.

Generally, by doing some overall research, it is possible to eliminate many of the software packages that don't meet your needs or that are too expensive, and create a list of accounting packages that are potentially a good fit for the organization.

After creating a list of potential packages, it's time to do more research. At this point, actually being able to see the software in action is helpful. Attending seminars offered by the vendor or a reseller of the products is a good way to see the system and ask key questions. However, remember that these people are trying to sell the product and are not likely to point out weaknesses or missing features. Some software companies will provide evaluation copies of their software, which is also a good way to test-drive the software. At this point, making a matrix of the product features and the organization's needs is helpful in narrowing the list of potential systems down to a few.

After developing a short list of systems to review, the next step is locating value-added resellers (VARs) to demonstrate the systems that the organization is interested in. Do not underestimate the importance of this step. Selecting the right VAR is critical to a successful implementation.

The software vendors can provide a list of resellers in the area. Be sure to get a list of resellers, not just one or two. It is then important to evaluate each reseller and determine whether they have the experience and ability to

Table 2.B.1
General System Questionnaire

General Ledger

- Number of organizations to be maintained on system
- Do the organizations need to be consolidated?
- Number of fiscal periods in each year
- How many historical years of information does the organization need to maintain?
- Languages needed
- Currencies needed
- What nonfinancial items need to be tracked (square footage, head count, etc.)?
- What regular allocations are performed?
  - Are they the same each time?
  - Do you allocate amounts based on the balance of other accounts?
- Number of transactions per year
- Number of accounts
- Account segmentation
  - Name of each segment and length
- Does the year close to one account or numerous divisional accounts?

Accounts Payable

- Number of vendors
- Number of invoices per month
- Frequency of check runs
- Recurring/monthly invoices
- Do you want to track any special information on each vendor?
- Is authorization needed to remove vendor holds or exceed maximum invoice amount?
- Are there natural divisions under which your vendors can be grouped?
- Do you use different check formats for different checking accounts?
- Do you want to track discounts available?
- Do you have default purchasing accounts for each vendor?
- What are your aging periods?
- Do you use credit cards to purchase items?
- What terms does your vendor offer you?
- Do you use purchase orders?
- Do you want to track encumbrances against budgets?
- Authorization needed to exceed budget amounts?

Accounts Receivable

- Number of customers
- Are there ways that you can divide your customers into classes that are similar?
- Statement frequency
- Do you accept credit cards from your customers?
- What terms do you offer?
- Do you want to track special information on your customers?
- Do you need to see a history of customer orders?

Inventory

- Number of inventory items
- Are any items combined together in "kits"?
- Do any products contain noninventory items (such as polybags)?
- Do you have matrix pricing (member, nonmember; early, late)?
- Do you need to track serial numbers?
- Do you want to show pictures of the item?
- Do you want to use bar code tracking?
- Is the inventory housed in multiple locations?

Project Costing (Grant Accounting)

- Number of projects
- Do you need to do project estimates on the system?
- Do you have scheduled (contract) payments?
- Do the contract draws need to be maintained?
- Do you have and time and materials billings?

Table 2.B.1   *(continued)*

- How many detail levels (projects/tasks/subtasks) are needed?
- What are the names and description of each level?
- Are there multiple funders for each project?
- Overhead/general and administrative (G&A) rate allocation?
- Tracking of individual hours and dollars
- In-kind contribution tracking

Payroll

- Number of employees
- Number of employee classes
- Do you use direct deposit?
- Do you maintain timesheet information?
- What timesheet reports are needed?
- What employee benefit information do you want to track?
- What human resources information do you want to track?

Order Entry/Registration

- Number of items or events
- Do you have matrix pricing (member, nonmember; early, late)?
- Do any of the items or events need to be grouped (like all national conference events)?
- Is there a need to be able to process credit cards within the order entry system?
- What kind of reports does the organization need to see (counts, picking tickets, etc.)

help evaluate the potential system and implement it if it is eventually chosen. One way to do this is to call and accumulate feedback on the reseller from local CPA firms or other similar organizations. Be sure to ask for at least three customer references with whom you can discuss their implementation process.

Consider the following criteria in selecting a VAR:

- The number and level of expertise of the consultants on staff (i.e., does the VAR have enough resources to service your account if a problem occurs?)
- The number of implementations performed by the VAR
- The number of support personnel
- The number of years the firm has been in business
- The number of years the consultants have dealt with the specific software

After identifying resellers for the products in which the organization is interested, an individualized demonstration should be arranged. The reseller should ask for much of the information that was completed in the initial questionnaire in order to better understand the organization's needs and specific goals. During the demonstration, ask about the average implementation time, the overall software customer base, and the support that is available through the reseller and the vendor.

After the demonstrations, it should be possible to narrow the list of possible accounting packages to three or fewer. At this point it would be useful to see some live implementations of the product. The software vendor should be able to provide a list of implementations in your area. At a minimum, call and ask about their experience with the software and their reseller. If possible, ask to see the software running on their site. This is often the best way to get some candid information about the system, its faults, and any problems with the reseller.

If at all possible, test the system with your own data. This may be possible if the reseller is willing to set up a test database environment for the organization at their site or if an evaluation copy of the software can be obtained. Testing with the organization's own information will help identify any key fields or processes that the software does not capture or do. In some cases, the system can be modified to capture this information—be sure to ask.

At the conclusion of this process, the organization should be in a good position to choose the best software package.

Implementation

After selecting the appropriate accounting software, the hard work of implementation begins. There are several steps to this process that your VAR should be able to help you through.

1. *Set up an implementation timeline and plan:* Once you've selected your VAR, sit down with them to establish an implementation timeline and plan. Your VAR should give you a list of the documents and information that they will need install your new system. Be prepared to allocate the time and staff necessary to quickly get this information together. Plan to spend time with the members of the team who will be responsible for the implementation. And be prepared to describe your processes and needs in considerable detail. The more you participate in this planning process, the smoother your implementation will be.

2. *Provide detailed documentation on procedures:* In addition to an accounting and policy manual, it's important to document the many idiosyncrasies of your operation. For instance, document where and how you code specific expenses, who and how often you bill, and how certain indirect expenses are recorded in the general ledger. The more documentation you can provide, the easier it will be to set-up the systems and processes in your new accounting package.

3. *Clean up your data:* Now is the time to get rid of those unused accounts, duplicate vendors, and ancient receivables. A cluttered general ledger just allows more room for mistakes and confusion. Eliminate these issues before they can become a problem.

4. *Redesign your chart of accounts:* Do not simply use your old account structure. Make sure to take advantage of all the features of your new software. You will probably have the ability to change your account segmentation, number and type of characters used, and roll-up reporting features. Give some thought as to what information you would like to get from the system and how that data should look. A well-designed chart of accounts can help take an organization to the next level and is crucial in determining what items, events, or programs are tracked.

5. *Give thought to the security issues:* Not everyone should have access to everything. Examine what each member of the staff does and what access they should have within the system. For nonaccounting users, thought should be given to providing an interface into the accounting system that will allow for easy viewing of information but provides no access to the actual accounting system.

6. *Prepare to test:* Don't expect to do live processing as soon as the system is up and running. Time needs to be devoted to testing the system to ensure that functions are running as expected and the system is producing the correct information. Providing feedback to the implementation team allows them to fix any problems before any live processing occurs. Make sure that testing includes a "load test"—that is, how does the system perform when everyone is on it at the same time. Although applications may work with one or two users, you need to understand how the system will operate when it is being used to capacity.

7. *Run parallel processing:* The ultimate test and proof that the new system is running correctly is to compare reports from both the new and old systems using the same data. Parallel processing needs to continue through at least the closing of one period. This will ensure that all the closing functions are working as well as the regular transaction processing. Staff members need to be assigned not only to enter in the data, but also to run reports and compare the data. Make sure your implementation plan includes the resources necessary for this step.

8. *Review how things have gone and revise:* This is an often forgotten but important step. Reviewing the problems encountered can help others on the implementation team avoid the same problems in their area. Also, the team is often able to come up novel solutions or workarounds as a team as opposed to an individual.

Appendix 2.C

Managing Funds and Understanding Relationships with Banking Institutions

Some of the key relationships established by any organization are those it makes with banking institutions. Banks can assist the organization in managing its cash and maximizing potential revenue. They are also key in assisting with periods of negative cash flow through the provision of a line of credit. It is therefore a good business practice to interview several institutions before deciding with which to form an alliance. Some of the items to consider are

- Does the institution have a separate division that caters to nonprofits?
- Does the institution offer special rates for nonprofit organizations?
- Will the institution have one representative who will manage the relationship?
- How many branches does the institution have, and where are they located?
- If there is no branch close to the organization, does the institution have a pick-up service?
- Does the bank have relationships with other institutions in other states, should your business take you there?
- What cash management products does the institution offer?
- What is the relationship between the bank and the credit card processing center (i.e., do they have their own center or do they use a third party)?
- What online services does the institution offer and what do they cost?
- What services are offered through the institution's lockbox service?
- Most organizations produce a request for proposal (RFP) as part of the investigatory process. In addition to providing the institution basic financial and transaction information, be sure to mention any specific requirements that the organization has. For instance, if the organization can only invest in government-backed securities for overnight investments, be sure that this is specified.

When establishing a new banking relationship, be sure to analyze your current accounts. Are there any accounts that can be combined or should be segregated? Some basic accounts the organization might consider are

- General operating
- Payroll (often a zero-balance account attached to the general operating account)
- Lockbox activity (for reconciliation ease, this is often a separate account)
- Credit card activity (again, for reconciliation ease)

In addition to these accounts, organizations often have agreements in place for short-term investment vehicles, such as overnight repurchase agreements (sweep accounts) and certificates of deposit. Depending on the specifics of the vehicle, this can help protect funds in excess of the FDIC limit as well as provide some operating revenue.

If the organization is not using sweep accounts for excess funds, the organization should ask the bank about providing a collateralized account with the Federal Reserve. Another method of providing this security is to use several financial institutions and keep less than the FDIC limit in each.

Conclusion

In conclusion, the process of selecting and implementing a new accounting system is a long and difficult one. However, with the proper planning, the process will result in a system that is well-suited to the organization's needs and will result in more comprehensive and useful information.

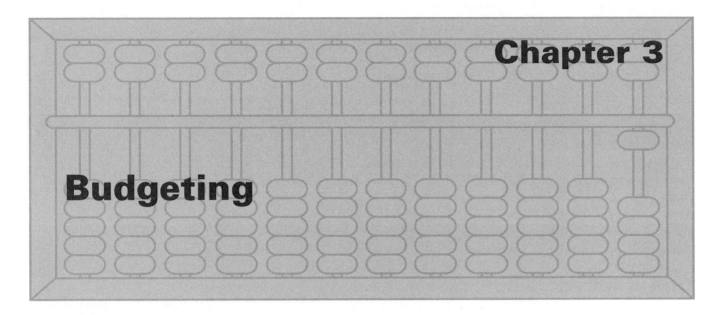

Chapter 3

Budgeting

Importance of Budgeting

Budgets force managers to become better administrators by making planning a priority. The budgeting process causes managers to focus on the future plans of their organization as well as the organization's past performance. Many people view budgets as a means to limit spending, but budgets should also be used to focus attention on company operations, allowing managers to plan and identify problems early. Budgets are used as benchmarks to compare actual performance with desired results. They serve as formal business plans by providing a plan for change rather than a reaction to it—they are a device to help organizations set goals and measure results.

Successful budgeting analyzes every significant item on the balance sheet and income statement. By spending time to prepare an accurate and thoughtful budget, an organization can meet both its long- and short-term strategic goals. Some of the advantages of budgeting are

- It provides a formal process for goal setting in both strategic and financial plans.
- Budgets provide concrete expectations and a framework to evaluate results.
- Budgets provide a mechanism for coordinating the different functions of an organization into a cohesive whole.

Prior to beginning the budget process, the organization needs to go through a separate business-planning process. This means that the organization must analyze prior-year results and examine the strategic plan from the board to determine what work needs to be accomplished in the upcoming year. The budget process can then take those plans and attach numbers. In many cases, the business plan may not have specific action items assigned. For instance, the business plan may call for increasing membership to 25,000 by 20XX. A general membership campaign may be defined under the plan but with no specific tasks. These tasks would need to be documented and defined under the budget process.

Budget Principles

To prepare a successful budget, management must

1. Clearly define its goals and objectives
2. Make goals realistic and reachable
3. Use historical data for projections
4. Understand the general business climate and economic conditions

5. Understand the condition of the industry
6. Define clear responsibility for forecasting costs

In addition, after the budget has been prepared, there must be a clear commitment to analyze actual results and make adjustments when unforeseen circumstances arise. For this reason, budgets must also be flexible so that they can change as conditions change.

Budgeted goals are a better basis for judging performance than are last year's actual results. One of the major drawbacks in using past actual results is that they fail to account for changes in economic conditions, business climate, technology changes, and the like. Budgets should also let managers know what is expected of them. Many people think of budgets only in terms of financial results, however budgets set the expectations for overall performance. For instance, in a training organization, the budget should establish the number and types of training courses that are to be held in a given year. It would also establish goals (and the funding) for developing new courses and delivery mechanisms. Ideally, managers should be involved in establishing the budget for their programs. This will help educate the manager as to the specifics of the program budget, get manager buy-in, and provide a more realistic budget scenario.

Types of Budgets

There are several different types of budgets used in nonprofits: operational budgets, capital budgets, and cash flow budgets.

Operational Budget

The operational budget identifies all the income and expenses needed by the organization in the upcoming year. Thus an operational budget would have the following components:

- Revenue budget—This should show the revenue from all sources, including dues, conference revenue, publication and product sales, investment income, contributions, grants, and any other revenue sources. In the nonprofit budget, it is necessary to categorize these revenues into restricted and nonrestricted sources.
- Expense (or purchases) budget—This budget should show all expenses broken down both by department and by functional category. Again, expenses should be divided into restricted and unrestricted categories.
- Budgeted statement of activities—The statement summarizes all the information from the revenue and expense budgets.

Operating budgets can be further subdivided into program and administrative budgets. Administrative budgets include programs such as fund-raising, facility costs, and general and administrative costs, whereas program budgets represent the cost of actual activities of the organization. Most programs in a nonprofit should be budgeted separately because these budgets will be used to raise individual support and funding.

Operational budgets should flow from the strategic and business plans. Start with listing all the goals that the organization established in the plans for the upcoming year. Individual tasks should be delineated beneath each of the goals and then individual elements should be delineated within each task. These elements can then be pulled together to create a budget with the functional elements. The following examples, Tables 3.1 and 3.2, show the basic elements of a strategic plan and the corresponding functional budget that was derived from it.

Capital Budget

The capital budget is used to help plan and manage projects that require large expenditures, for example, purchasing equipment or making improvements to an organization's space. Capital budgets may be for a single year or for multiple years, as in construction projects. Basically, there are two types of capital budgets:

- Capital improvements budget—This budget reflects expenses for major, nonrecurring expenses, such as the construction or renovation of facilities or the purchase of major equipment or systems.
- Capital equipment budget—This budget is for the purchase of furniture, equipment, or other items with useful lives longer than 1 year.

Table 3.1 Example 1—Strategic Plan

Strategic Plan for Membership Department: Provide Quality Customer Service to Members

Respond to member inquiries and requests within 1 business day		
	Telephone	6,000
	Membership database	136,800
Membership fulfillment		
	Prospective member kit mailings	
	Postage	750
	Roster, single invoice, replacement membership card requests	
	Printing	2,500
	Postage	2,500
	Supplies	1,000
	Renewal notice mailings	
	Dues invoices	
	Printing	2,250
	Postage	20,000
	Design fees	2,000
	New member kit/membership card mailing (presentation folders, membership cards, etc.)	
	Printing	10,000
	Postage	20,000
	Design fees	5,000
Increase the total number of members to 25,000		
Membership retention		
	Local workshops (10 visits)	
	Travel	9,500
	Airfare $500	500
	Hotel $300	300
	Food $150	150
	Printing	500
	Postage	250
	Shipping	250
	Supplies	250
	Direct member mailing	
	Printing	1,000
	Postage	3,500
Member recruitment		
	Membership campaign	
	Update membership brochure	
	Printing	5,000
	Postage	1,000
	Design fees	1,000
	Professional fees (development)	5,000
Monthly telephone status call		
	Telephone	600
Receive training to increase membership satisfaction		
	Training	1,500
	Travel	1,500
	Supplies	1,500
		241,150
	Salaries and benefits	116,866
		358,016

Table 3.2   Example 2—Functional Program Budget

	Proposed Budget FY2003
Membership	
Salaries and fringe benefits	116,866
Postage and shipping	48,250
Printing and duplicating	21,250
Telephone	6,600
Supplies	2,750
Staff training	1,500
Travel	11,000
Database fees	136,800
Design fees	8,000
Professional fees	5,000
Subtotal membership	$358,016

The effect of the capital budget must be taken into consideration when preparing the operating budget. For example, the amount of depreciation expense must be noted in the general administration of the organization. Similarly, any plans to finance a capital project must also be taken into consideration. Table 3.3 shows a sample capital budget, and Table 3.4 shows depreciation over 3 years.

Cash Flow Budget

The cash flow budget shows the cash inflows and outflows for a specified period of time, or, more simply stated, it is the cash received from revenues and cash spent for all items, such as expenses, loan repayments, and equipment. Generally, this budget is produced after the operational and capital budgets have been produced. This budget is important to complete in order to determine whether there is enough cash to meet the obligations of the organization.

All budgets, including the program budgets and the operating budget, affect the cash flow budget. In addition, the capital expenditures and plans for long-term debt financing also affect the cash budget.

Table 3.3   Example 3—Sample Capital Budget

Project Title: Renovating New Office Space

Project Items	Total Budget	20XX Budget	20X1 Budget
Signage	$2,000	$2,000	$0
Demolition	$25,000	$25,000	$0
Architectural fees	$10,000	$5,000	$5,000
Telephone system	$10,000	$0	$10,000
Furniture refinishing	$5,000	$0	$5,000
Cabling and wiring	$5,000	$5,000	$0
Construction	$50,000	$25,000	$25,000
TOTALS	$107,000	$62,000	$45,000

Table 3.4   Example 4—Depreciation

Capital Item	Depreciation 20XX	Depreciation 20X1	Depreciation 20X2
Renovating office space, year 1	$3,100	$6,200	$6,200
Renovating office space, year 2		$2,250	$4,500
	$3,100	$8,450	$10,700

Note: This example is based on a 10-year lease observing a half-year convention.

The cash flow budget projects cash inflows (receipts) and cash outflows (disbursements) on a month-by-month basis over the entire fiscal year. By performing this analysis, it is possible to identify when projected disbursements will exceed the cash on hand (negative cash flow) or when cash will be available for short-term investment (positive cash flow). Example 5, Table 3.5 shows a portion of a cash flow budget.

The ultimate goal of cash flow budgeting is to determine whether or not the cash position will fall below the organization's minimum cash balance. The size of the organization's minimum cash balance depends on how accurately staff can predict when cash payments are due and how much cash the staff believes should be kept in reserve.

In addition to doing a cash flow budget, it is important to do cash flow projections on a monthly basis. This should be done on a regular basis, not just when a cash crisis occurs. Management must identify periods of negative cash flow in order to identify steps necessary to prevent interruption of programs and services. This action is also critical in planning investment decisions and the timing for the maturity of funds. For instance, an organization may choose not to reinvest dividends or coupon payments received on investments if the cash flow budget projects a low cash balance. Or, an organization may time bond maturity dates to coincide with periods of low cash balances.

Problems can occur in cash flow funding. For instance, many grants and contracts reimburse the organization only after the expenses have been incurred. Or, oftentimes the organization must expend funds for an upcoming event without having received any registration income. In order to prepare for these situations, nonprofits must accurately project cash flow in order to ensure sufficient available cash.

During periods of negative cash flow, an organization must increase its flow of revenue, decrease its expense flow, or both. Some possible ways to do this are

- Becoming more active in the collection of outstanding receivables
- Delaying major purchases
- Freezing hiring and staff salary increases
- Implementing new ideas for development and fund-raising
- Establishing payment plans with vendors
- Reducing expenses
- Utilizing a line of credit
- Transferring cash from reserves

Table 3.5 Example 5—Cash Flow Budget

	January	February	March
Estimated cash receipts from			
Contributions	$150,000	$100,000	$125,000
Event receipts	50,000	10,000	20,000
Publication sales	5,000	5,000	5,000
Grants	0	100,000	0
Loan proceeds	50,000		
Other (interest, investment gains, etc.)	4,000	4,000	4,000
Total cash receipts	$259,000	$219,000	$189,000
Estimated cash disbursements for			
Operating expenditures	$208,000	$157,000	$187,000
Capital expenditures	10,000	0	5,000
Loan repayment	0	1,014	1,014
Total cash disbursements	$218,000	$158,014	$193,014
Cash increase (decrease)	$41,000	$60,986	($4,014)
Beginning cash balance	50,000	91,000	151,986
Ending cash balance	$91,000	$151,986	$147,972

Some of these items such as A/R collection, new ideas for development, expense reductions, and utilizing a line of credit, are generally ongoing activities used to boost short-term cash liquidity. However, some items such as hiring freezes, delaying major purchases, payment plans with vendors, and using cash from reserves are generally steps taken only when cash is particularly tight. When reviewing these more extreme options, be aware that there are consequences—some of which may be severe. For instance, delaying a major purchase or program implementation may have revenue consequences in the future. Cutting services to funders or members may have a negative impact on the image of the organization and engender feelings of ill will. Hiring freezes may cause concern among employees and lead to further eroding of the staff. All of these tactics may also lead to concerns regarding the financial viability of the organization and ultimately lead to a loss in customer confidence. As such, a loss could result in the ultimate demise of an organization; serious thought should be given before using extreme measures to boost cash.

Budget Implementation

The following sections outline some of the steps necessary in preparing a budget.

Step 1—Deciding Responsibilities and Timelines

The first step of the budget process is to establish what each person's responsibility is in the budget process:

- Who is responsible for preparing the budget templates and worksheets?
- Who is responsible for preparing budget estimates?
- What is each manager's role in the budget process?

The second part of this step is to develop the budget calendar. In this process, the specific timeframes and overall process is determined. Specific budget tasks can be determined as well as each person's role in those tasks. Remember that time for budget review and adjustments must also be included in the budget calendar. Table 3.6 is an example of a budget calendar.

Step 2—Prepare the Budget Package

Many managers are intimidated by the budget process. The purpose of the budget package is to make this task easier for them. Included in this package should be last year's budget, which can serve as a reminder as to what items were included in the previous budget:

Table 3.6 Sample Budget Calendar

Deadline	Task	Person Responsible
10/1	Meet to establish strategic goals and tasks	CEO, CFO, department managers
10/15	Meeting to pass out and review budget package with department managers	CFO
	Salary allocations and fringe benefit allocations due	CFO
11/08	Program plan due from department managers	Department managers
11/15	Department managers prepare program budgets according to program plan	Department managers
11/21	Consolidate program budgets into organizational budget	CFO and finance staff
11/30	Management reviews budget and discusses revisions with department managers	CEO, CFO, and department managers
12/7	Prepare final version of budget	CFO and finance staff
12/15	Present budget to board of directors	CFO
12/23	Incorporate all board of director changes to the budget	CFO
12/31	Distribute final budget to all staff	CFO

1. The budget calendar
2. Blank program plan
3. Blank budget forms
4. Any overall budget assumptions that are being made based on economic or business conditions

Step 3—Estimate Income

For various reasons, estimating income is more difficult than projecting expenses. In some cases, the nonprofit has a chance of receiving income but has no firm commitment. For instance, grant applications may be pending or revenue may be anticipated from contribution drives but not yet pledged. The effects of new campaigns, the economy, and past historical experience must also be taken into account.

Because of the many variables involved, when preparing income estimates, it is important to clearly document the assumptions used. Documenting assumptions is also useful when it is necessary to make budget adjustments and when presenting the budget to others. There are several sources that can be used for projecting income:

- Actual income from historical sources
- Payment schedules from grants and contracts
- Collection schedules and rates
- Estimated number of program participants
- Fee schedules
- Inclination or declination rates (e.g., what's the average rate that membership been increasing or decreasing over the past 5 years)

Step 4—Prepare the Program Budgets

Expense budgets should be built to stay within the amount of revenue budgeted. This usually means developing the expense budget for all the program activities and then prioritizing the activities based on the strategic plan and revenue available.

There are five basic steps to preparing a program budget:

1. Prepare a list of goals for the department.
2. Identify specific activities to be performed under each goal.
3. Determine the individual elements necessary to carry out each activity.
4. Determine the costs of each element.
5. Prepare the department budget.

Step 4-1

To prepare a program budget, the department manager first must list what goals the department is responsible for achieving. A list of goals for a membership department might look like Table 3.7.

Table 3.7 Membership Department Goals

1. Respond to member inquiries within 24 hours.
2. Provide up-to-date membership information to the board of directors.
3. Send dues renewal invoices in a timely manner.
4. Increase the total number of members by 10%.
5. Provide each member with information regarding benefits and programs available.
6. Increase overall membership satisfaction to 90% as measured by the satisfaction survey.

Step 4-2

Each goal should then be expanded to include individual programs or activities. For instance, the membership goals might be expanded to include the following:

1. Increase the total number of members by 10%.
   a. Have "Be a member, get a member" campaign.
   b. Purchase five new mailing lists and send membership brochures.
   c. Have booths at two trade shows.

Step 4-3

Each program or activity can then be expanded to include individual elements:

1. Increase the total number of members by 10%.
   a. Have "Be a member, get a member" campaign.
      - Printing of flyer
      - Envelopes for flyer
      - Postage to mail flyer
      - Prize money
   b. Purchase five new mailing lists and send membership brochures.
      - Mailing list purchase
      - Printing of brochures
      - Design fees for brochures
      - Envelopes for brochures
      - Postage
   c. Have booths at a two trade shows.
      - Booth fees
      - Printing of booth materials
      - Shipping of display
      - Booth prizes
      - Booth supplies

Steps 4-4 and 4-5

Values can then be assigned to each activity element, resulting in a table similar to Table 3.1. Lines within this department plan can then be added to derive the entire budget for the particular natural account.

1. Increase the total number of members by 10%.
   a. Have "Be a member, get a member" campaign.
      - Printing of flyer $500
      - Envelopes for flyer $500
      - Postage to mail flyer
      - Prize money
   b. Purchase mailing lists and send membership brochures.
      - Mailing list purchase
      - Printing of brochures $500
      - Design fees for brochures

- Envelopes for brochures $500
- Postage
c. Have booth at two trade shows.
  - Booth fees
  - Printing of booth materials $500
  - Shipping of display
  - Booth prizes
  - Booth supplies
Total Printing: $2,500

Composing a budget in this manner is more time-consuming, however if budget reductions need to be made, it can be done by removing specific activities and all of the associated cost rather than just making "blanket" cuts. This is advantageous because it forces management to prioritize activities and understand what functions they cannot perform within the year.

Step 5—Allocate Overhead and Shared Costs

Costs that benefit more than one program but cannot be correlated to specifically one function within the organization are called indirect or overhead costs. Examples of these costs would be the accounting department's operation, development costs, and the cost of senior management. These items are typically allocated to the other program department on some predetermined basis. Shared costs are those items or services that are shared among departments, such as phones, postage, and duplicating.

In order to show the true cost of a program, it is important to allocate these costs in a rational and justifiable manner. The following are common allocation methods:

- Fringe benefit costs can be allocated based upon the percentage of salaries in each individual department.
- A log (either electronic or paper) can be created for items such as postage, copying, and telephone. Many companies offer electronic tracking for these expenses by department at little or no cost.
- Space and facilities costs can be allocated based on the square feet each department or person occupies.

General and administrative (G&A) and accounting costs can be allocated based on a department's percentage of the total budget. An example of allocating G&A costs follows in Table 3.8. Allocating the accounting and G&A departments results in Table 3.9.

It should be noted that grants or contracts might subject the allocations to limits. Additionally, all allocation methodologies should be documented and periodically reviewed. Some people would argue that allocating overhead expenses within the budget is not necessary. This is based on the fact that managers cannot be held accountable for indirect costs allocated to their department. It should be noted, however, that indirect expense allocation is necessary in order to show the full cost of any program and to understand the use of shared resources.

Table 3.8   Allocation of G&A Costs Based on Percentage of Total Budget

Expense Budget		Percentage of Direct Budget
Membership	$112,000	21.9%
Meetings	$200,000	39.0%
National conference	$150,000	29.3%
Publications	$50,000	9.8%
Subtotal direct program expenses	$512,000	
Accounting	$100,000	
G&A	$200,000	
Total Budget	$812,000	

Table 3.9 Allocation of Costs for G&A and Accounting Departments

Expense Budget	Direct Expenses	Accounting	G&A	Total
Membership	$112,000	$21,900	$43,800	$177,700
Meetings	$200,000	$39,000	$78,000	$317,000
National conference	$150,000	$29,300	$58,600	$237,900
Publications	$50,000	$9,800	$19,600	$79,400
Total Budget	$512,000	$100,000	$200,000	$812,000

Step 6—Total Organizational Budget

The next step in the budget process is to prepare the total organizational budget. This budget serves as the primary document that the board and others will view. This document should summarize all income and expenses into broad categories and may include comparative data to help the reader understand the changes that have taken place in the current year. Table 3.10 shows an example of an organizational budget.

Step 7—Budget Notes

After completing the budget, a summary should be written which lists all of the budget assumptions. Things to be included are changes in personnel (new positions, positions eliminated, salary increases, etc.), changes in department goals and policies, explanations of new programs, and a list of the assumptions used in preparing the budget. An example of a budget summary for an organization with two sites is listed in the next section.

Budget Summary

OVERALL   The total expense budget for FY20XX is $4,500,400 and that number includes $1,500,800 of in-kind expenses. This would leave $2,999,600 in cash expenses. Table 3.11 summarizes this information.

EXPENSES   The largest expense items incurred by the organization are salaries and fringe benefits. For FY03 salaries are budgeted at $1,411,700 and fringe benefits at $302,800. In FY02 these figures were $978,100 and $210,400, respectively. The bulk of the increase in salaries is from the addition of personnel, totaling $388,300. In general, salaries were computed using a 2% COLA amount and small merit increases. All nonpersonnel expenses were computed by increasing FY02 estimated expenses by 3% (rounded to the nearest $100) except for certain fixed expenses that were increased based on contracts already in place. Development costs have been split between the two sites based on the percentage of revenue each site has to raise.

REVENUES   Increases in revenue are based on FY02's estimated total revenue of $2,750,000, plus an 8% increase which matches the average revenue growth over the last 5 years, plus a 2% increase projected as new revenue sources directly related to new work. The net 10% increase results in a budgeted cash revenue of $ 3,025,000.

Notice that notes outlining the major assumptions used or changes made to the budget are outlined in the summary. A complete list of assumptions for each functional expense category should be included in the budget notes.

In addition to this executive summary, detailed notes should be prepared that explain each item at either a programmatic or functional level. The following list is an example of budget notes:

Operating Fund Expenses

Salaries and fringe benefits: Salaries and wages in each department reflect anticipated wages for FY2004 allocated among the departments as recently recalculated according to a timesheet study for the past 5 months of activity. This category also includes two new positions: operations position and a membership director. A cost factor of 25% is used to calculate benefit cost.

Postage and delivery: Normal postage expense associated with each department based on actual usage.

Membership: Membership costs reflect costs of mailing renewal dues notices, membership fulfillment supplies, new member kits, and so on.

Table 3.10 ABC Membership Organization Proposed Budget for the Year Ended December 31, 20XX

	Office Management	Information Technology	Development	Governance	Public Policy	Membership	National Conference	Meetings	Totals	FY20XX-1 Totals	Net Change
Revenue											
Net membership dues						1,300,000			1,300,000	1,200,000	100,000
Corporate affiliates	100,000		100,000						200,000	150,000	50,000
Administrative revenue	35,000								35,000	32,510	2,490
National conference							350,000		350,000	300,000	—
50,000											
Registration & events								85,000	85,000	85,000	—
Advertising & subscriptions			25,000						25,000	25,000	—
Investment income	25,000								25,000	22,550	2,450
Total Revenue	160,000	—	125,000	—	—	1,300,000	350,000	85,000	2,020,000	1,815,060	204,940
Expenses											
Salaries & fringe benefits	65,000	31,250	40,000	26,000	535,000	117,000	20,000	15,000	849,250	861,968	(12,718)
Postage & delivery	2,500	—	—	1,000	10,229	44,750	17,100	5,000	80,579	54,474	26,106
Printing & duplicating	—	—	1,000	7,500	9,100	39,950	23,200	3,500	84,250	60,070	24,181
Supplies	8,750		—	2,000	1,500	1,500	6,000	4,000	23,750	11,414	12,336
Telephone	3,000	4,610	1,000	5,000	2,500	6,600	2,150	500	25,360	14,425	10,936
Travel	5,000		—	38,500	6,500	1,500	13,000	1,000	65,500	15,064	50,437
Audit fees	13,000								13,000	12,877	123
Depreciation	31,000								31,000	30,996	4
Dues & subscriptions	250	400			4,550			850	6,050	5,328	722
Insurance	30,000								30,000	4,407	25,593
Legal fees	8,000								8,000	13,475	(5,475)
Maintenance & repair	7,900								7,900	1,529	6,372
Office rent	150,000								150,000	115,953	34,047
Service agreements	35,000								35,000	35,000	—
Computer maintenance		15,000							15,000	15,467	(467)
Professional fees			40,000	5,400			43,000	5,400	93,800	100,000	(6,200)
Staff recruitment	500								500	100	400
CEO expense	5,000								5,000	5,000	—
Staff training		2,800			1,650	1,500		17,200	23,150	785	22,365
Taxes	4,000								4,000	4,000	—
Bank fees/credit processing	15,000								15,000	29,996	(14,996)
Web page						35,000			35,000	9,365	25,636
Audio/visual				6,500			33,000		39,500	35,000	4,500
Temporary help					2,000				2,000	2,500	(500)
Software		9,000							9,000	5,000	4,000
Computer supplies		1,160							1,160	1,000	160
Computer repairs		4,750							4,750	5,000	(250)
Design fees					4,000				4,000	3,000	1,000
Total expenses	383,900	68,970	82,000	91,900	577,029	247,800	157,450	52,450	1,661,499	1,453,188	208,311
Net Revenue (Expense)	(223,900)	(68,970)	43,000	(91,900)	(577,029)	1,052,200	192,550	32,550	358,501	361,872	(3,371)

Table 3.11   Total Expense Budget for FY20XX

	Total Expenses	In-Kind Expenses	Cash Expenses
Site 1	$3,500,400	$1,300,800	$2,199,600
Site 2	1,000,000	200,000	800,000
Total	4,500,400	1,500,800	2,999,600

National conference: Postage for marketing piece, freight and storage of supplies/goods.

Public policy: Postage for increased awareness mailings and regular communications with members.

Communications: Postage for public-relations mailings and specific communications to the membership.

Printing and duplicating: Represents costs of direct copy jobs purchased by the department. The cost of the copier lease is included in the service agreement line item.

Membership: Printing of renewal invoices and envelopes, state activity reports, new member kits, prospective member mailings, brochures, new state membership kits, and charters.

National conference: Copier and fax rental and all duplicating (board book, tickets, ballots, motion forms, confirmation packets, and various handouts) required at national conference before and on-site.

Office management: Miscellaneous printing of letterhead, envelopes, portfolios, mailing labels, and so on.

Supplies: Office supplies and noncapitalized furniture and fixtures.

Telephone: Local and long-distance charges. Expenses in this category now include the cost of two T-1 lines into the office and the cost of increased conference calls (as opposed to travel).

In addition to the proposed budget, a budget summary, budget notes, charts, and graphs are often used to aid readers in understanding the budget. These charts might include a comparison of the proposed budget to actual expenses, a graph showing membership trends, or any other presentation that might assist a reader in understanding the background used in developing the budget.

Step 8—Board Review and Approval

The final step in the budgeting process is the review and approval by the board of directors. Some boards delegate the responsibility of budget overview to subcommittees such as a finance or budget committee; others review the budget directly. Because of their strategic role in the organization's business plan, the individuals who review the budget have the potential to offer useful feedback in the budget process.

Budget Monitoring

In order to have an effective monitoring system, the monthly financial statements must be compared to the operating budget on a regular basis. The budget is the yardstick by which managers are able to assess progress and identify expense overruns and income shortfalls. With early identification of these problems, steps can be taken to correct the problems.

It is the responsibility of the CFO to prepare monthly reports that compare the actual expenditures to the budget. Variances should be identified, and managers should be able to explain the differences beyond a certain percentage or dollar amount. The CFO and manager should then work together to develop a corrective action plan for any items identified as being potentially problematic in the future.

Budget Modification

A budget represents the management's best estimates for the future at a specific moment in time. Because circumstances change, such as adding new programs or eliminating funding, it is often necessary to modify the budget to reflect these changes.

A document establishing the budget modification process should be developed by management and should contain a timeline. Budget modifications should be made only at specified times of the year, not on a continual basis. A clear timeline indicating when budget modifications are to be submitted to accounting for consideration should be provided. These instructions should also provide clear guidance on who has the authority to approve budget modifications.

Conclusion

Budgets guide an organization's plans to use its financial and human resources. They are an effective monitoring tool and a map of how to reach the organization's goals while fulfilling its mission. An effective, well-planned budget process will help the organization prepare a good budget.

Good budgeting is the basis for understanding the organization and the environment it operates in. Budgets help analyze strengths and weaknesses, identify successes and failures, and provide an opportunities for the organization to evaluate itself.

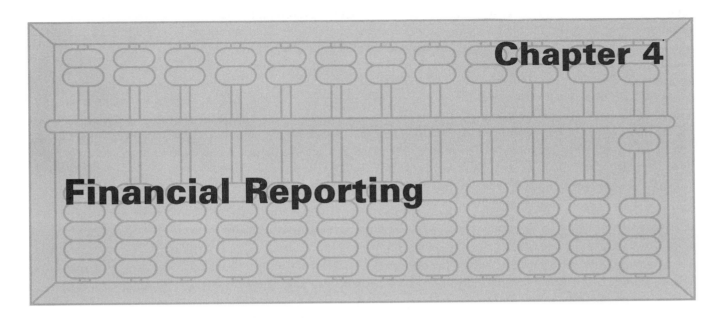

Chapter 4

Financial Reporting

Like any business, nonprofit organizations need to prepare financial statements on a monthly basis. Internal financial statements are generated monthly so that managers can monitor the program activities and make any necessary adjustments to the operation or to expenses.

Although similar in many ways to any business, there are some special requirements when reporting for nonprofit entities. The Financial Accounting Standards Board (FASB) has issued Statement of Financial Accounting Standard (SFAS) #117, which addresses some of these differences. The provisions of this statement set consistent standards and terminology when preparing nonprofit financial statements. When producing monthly statements, it is not necessary to comply with all the provisions of SFAS #117, although, for consistency purposes, some conformity (for instance keeping the same asset and liability classes) is recommended.

Internal financial statements, at a minimum, should include the following:

- The statement of financial position
- The statement of activities
- Individual department or program statements

Unlike audited financial statements, internal statements do not usually contain a statement of cash flows or financial statement notes.

Generally, internal financial statements are generated around the middle of the following month from the month being reported. For example, July 31 financial statements would be completed around August 15. This allows the necessary time to collect all bank and investment statements and for those statements to be reconciled. Once the internal statements are produced, they can be delivered to the executive committee and CEO (or to whomever approves them in your organization) to review. Following all necessary reviews and corrections, the statements can be released to other parties as specified by the officers.

Statement of Financial Position

Previously known as the balance sheet, this statement focuses on the financial position of the entire organization at a particular moment in time. The statement of financial position enumerates the total assets, liabilities, and net assets of the organization and provides important information about an organization's liquidity.

Within the statement of financial position, assets and liabilities are grouped into like categories. It is recommended that a classified balance sheet be presented, on which current assets and current liabilities are displayed separately from other assets and liabilities. The current classification would generally apply to those assets that will be realized in cash, sold, or consumed within 1 year and those liabilities that will be discharged by use of current assets or the creation of other current liabilities within 1 year. Assets and liabilities are also presented in order of their nearness of conversion to cash, and liabilities are sequenced according to the nearness of their maturity and resulting use of cash. Within the statement of financial position, assets and liabilities are grouped into like categories, such as cash and cash equivalents, accounts and notes receivable, inventories, deposits and prepaids, marketable securities, and other investment assets held. Another grouping would be long-lived assets, such as land, buildings, and equipment. However, one area that is specifically different from commercial enterprises is the area of restricted cash. Restricted cash and assets should not be shown as part of the current assets of the organization. It should be shown in a separate category, such as other assets, so as not to distort the organization's financial ratios.

The equivalent of the owner's equity portion of the balance sheet in a commercial enterprise is the net assets section of the statement of financial position. As discussed in a previous chapter, there can be three different types of net assets:

- Unrestricted net assets
- Temporarily restricted net assets
- Permanently restricted net assets

Unrestricted net assets are the assets that are derived as the result of operations (i.e., revenues less expenses) of the organization or from expired restrictions on other contributions. They can be used for any purpose the organization designates at any time.

Restricted net assets, on the other hand, are assets given to the organization that have some donor-imposed restrictions placed on them. These restrictions are further broken down into those that are temporary and those that are permanent. A permanent restriction is one in which the original asset must be kept in perpetuity. In the case of cash or an investment, it can be used to derive income, but the original corpus of the gift must be kept intact. With a temporarily restricted net asset, the asset can be used (or sold) but only for a specific purpose or once a time restriction has elapsed.

Statement of Activities

This statement is similar to the profit and loss statement of a commercial enterprise because it reflects the revenues, expenses, and the resulting net increase or decrease in net assets. Often the activity for each group or class of assets is shown in separate columns. In this manner it is possible to see the effect of operations on all three classes of assets.

One of the primary purposes of this statement is to show the primary sources of revenue for the organization and how the organization uses its resources to carry out the mission of the organization. Further, this should allow the reader of the financial statement to determine the organization's performance during the period.

Program Statements

Not generally included in the audited financial statements, program statements give the specific detail of each individual program or project. These statements might be subtotaled further into operating divisions or operational sites where work is conducted. Within each program statement are the natural expense accounts that are related to that specific program. Other information that is generally provided on these statements is the budget for each of the natural accounts and an actual to budget variance column. This information provides department managers with the information necessary to control and monitor programmatic problems or to identify and celebrate good things that happen so they can be understood and replicated, if possible.

Financial Ratio Analysis

Another purpose of the financial statements is to compare the organization to other similar nonprofit organizations. One method of measuring an organization's performance is to calculate financial ratios. Ratios show relative value rather than just empirical information and can be used to compare performance against goals, past and present performance, and identify unfavorable trends. Ratio analysis should be performed consistently for several successive years in order to identify early warning indications or problems. It is not a one-time tool.

Balance-Sheet Ratios

Ratios applied to the statement of financial position (or balance sheet) measure the organization's ability to meet its current obligations (liquidity ratios) with its resources and reveal the extent to which the organization is reliant on credit (leverage ratios). The most common liquidity ratios include the current ratio, quick ratio, and working capital.

Current Ratio

The current ratio measures the ability of an organization to pay its current debts with its current assets, allowing for a margin of safety. This ratio is calculated as follows:

$$\text{Current ratio} = \frac{\text{Total current assets}}{\text{Total current liabilities}}$$

A generally acceptable current ratio is 2:1, meaning that the organization has twice the amount of current assets as current liabilities. An organization would want to maintain this level in order to pay all their current debts and still have enough assets left to survive for a period of time. A minimum acceptable level is 1:1, although this allows for no margin of safety.

Quick Ratio

The following calculation is used for the quick ratio:

$$\text{Quick ratio} = \frac{\text{Current assets} - \text{Inventory and prepaids}}{\text{Total current liabilities}}$$

This ratio is sometimes called the "acid-test" ratio and is one of the best measures of liquidity. It measures the truly liquid assets with relatively stable values. A generally acceptable quick ratio is 1:1.

Working Capital

Working capital is calculated as follows:

$$\text{Working capital} = \text{Total current assets} - \text{Total current liabilities}$$

Similar to the current ratio, this calculation measures the amount of cash flow available to the organization. In arranging financing, this calculation is often reviewed to determine the borrower's ability to repay the debt.

Leverage Ratio

This ratio measures how reliant an organization is on debt financing rather than its own unrestricted net assets. In other words, creditors will perceive an organization as a high risk the higher the liabilities are in relationship to its net assets. In a nonprofit organization, this is further limited by the nature (restricted versus unrestricted) of those assets. Although not officially defined anywhere, we have chosen to present this ratio using only unrestricted net assets in the denominator because restricted net assets may not be available to cover liabilities:

$$\text{Leverage ratio} = \frac{\text{Total liabilities}}{\text{Total Unrestricted assets}}$$

Reserve Ratio

The reserve ratio is intended to calculate what percentage of the association's annual budget is covered by available assets. The following equation is used to calculate this ratio:

$$\text{Reserve ratio} = \frac{\text{Expandable net assets}}{\text{Total annual expenses}}$$

Exactly what assets should be considered expendable net assets is a much debated topic. One possible answer is that expendable net assets equals total *unrestricted* net assets minus the net investment in fixed assets plus *temporarily restricted* net assets available to meet a portion of the next year's expenses.

Income Statement Ratios

Ratios applied to the income statement (i.e., statement of activities) generally measure the profitability of an organization. One common misconception is that a nonprofit organization cannot make a profit. Nonprofits can make a profit; these profits, however, are not returned to the board or investors but rather reinvested in the organization to provide more services. Thus income statement ratios are still useful in analyzing the operations (activities) for a nonprofit.

Net Profit Ratio

The net profit ratio measures the return on revenue after all expenses have been subtracted or, in other words, the percentage of revenue left after accounting for all expenses. Nonprofit organizations generally do not pay income taxes, so it is not necessary to adjust this ratio for taxes as it is in a commercial enterprise.

$$\text{Net profit ratio} = \frac{\text{Revenue} - \text{Expenses}}{\text{Revenue}}$$

Return of Assets Ratio

The return of assets ratio measures the efficiency of the net revenue generated from assets. In other words, it measures the amount of net revenue that can be generated for each dollar invested by the organization. This ratio is calculated as follows:

$$\text{Return on assets} = \frac{\text{Change in net assets (Net revenue)}}{\text{Total assets}}$$

Using these financial ratios, nonprofit boards can identify trends and compare their organization's progress with others. This also allows boards to assess the relative strengths and weaknesses of the organization and build business plans to meet the organization's needs. Organizations typically compare their results to the ASAE Operating Ratio Report, which shows financial statistics for various associations.

Revenue per Staff Member

The revenue per staff member ratio gives a picture of the efficiency of the staff in generating revenue. Straight comparisons to other organizations must be modified depending on the type of organization you are (e.g., individual membership or corporate membership) and a host of other factors. This rate would be calculated as follows:

$$\frac{\text{Total revenue}}{\text{Total number of staff}}$$

The Financial Statement Process

As important as producing the financial statements are the process and controls used to generate them. A closing process should be developed by the accounting staff, which ensures that all adjustments and entries have been recorded prior to producing the financial statements. Some typical adjustments needed at the end of the month include

- Reconciling all cash accounts and making necessary journal entries for bank charges and interest earned
- Reconciling investments in order to record interest and gains or losses to the portfolio
- Recording the monthly depreciation allocation
- Releasing temporarily restricted funds that have monthly expiration
- Making proper entries to accounts receivable at month-end for monies that have been promised in future periods
- Making adjustments to prepaid expense accounts as the monthly expense is incurred
- Allocating expenses by departments, such as telephone, salary, and postage expenses
- Reviewing all expense accounts to ensure that items were recorded properly when originally posted to the general ledger
- Allocating any miscellaneous expenses to proper departments or programs
- Allocating general and administrative expenses to individual departments or programs (often only done at year-end)

The checklist in Table 4.1 is an example of one commonly used in producing financial statements.

Table 4.1 USA Membership Organization

Checklist	Target Date	Completed By	Date Completed	Reviewed By	Date Reviewed
Weekly					
Collect, open, sort, and distribute invoices (Monday/Thursday)					
Process checks and file (Wednesday)					
Input payables into accounting system (Wednesday)					
Process credit cards (Monday/Tuesday/Friday)					
Batch checks and other receivables (Monday/Tuesday/Thursday/Friday)					
Input cash receipts into Great Plains (Monday)					
Log receivable batches into IMIS (daily with batching)					
Meet with CEO to give updates and check signatures					
Biweekly					
Process payroll (Monday)					
Payroll JE (Thursday)					
Distribute, copy, and file payroll (Thursday)					
Monthly					
Membership month-end processing					
Direct dues cash summary JE					
Process refund checks for individual members					
Process refund checks for states					
Update membership committee spreadsheet					
Cash reconciliation					
Checking account 1					
Checking account 2					
Investment reconciliation					
Operating investments					
Endowment account					
Permanently restricted reserve					
Receivables reviewed for bad debt					
Interest receivable—adjust monthly					
Prepaid expenses					
Allocate postage					
Allocate insurance					
Depreciation					
Monthly allocation					
Accruals					
Payroll withholdings					
Accrued salaries					
Accrued leave					
Accrued legal invoices					
Accounts Payable					
Subledger reviewed					
Deferrals					
Def dues schedule prep					
Dues allocated					
Dues refundable—state reviewed					
Other					
Office supplies expense—reasonable					

Presenting Financial Information to the Board and Finance Committee

After the financial statements have been produced, they are generally distributed to department managers and other internal staff. On at least a quarterly basis, a condensed version of the statements should be sent to the finance committee. Also financial information is generally reviewed whenever the board of directors meets.

It is important to provide this information to the board and finance committee on a regular basis so that the board can make informed decisions. However, the challenge is presenting financial information in a way that the board can understand—particularly if the board has members who are not well acquainted with financial information.

In general, the Board is not interested in specific numbers. That is to say that they are more interested in the trends of the numbers. Is revenue increasing or decreasing? How are expenses in comparison to budget? Where are we having trouble containing expenses?

One good way to present financial information is to use graphics. Microsoft PowerPoint and Excel both have excellent graphic utilities. Some suggestions follow for presenting the various parts of the financial statement.

An excellent way of presenting the statement of activities is by using pie charts. Pie charts show the relationships between numbers. For instance, if the statement of activities shows that fully three quarters of the organization's assets are in investments, this point could be made much clearer by using a pie chart rather than by simply displaying the statement of activities.

A pie chart can also be an effective way of demonstrating the net assets of the organization and its relationship to liabilities. Using a pie chart in a presentation, one could make the following statement: "From the graph above, it is possible to see that the true debts of the organization, accounts payable, are relatively small and that the total liabilities of the organization are less than its net assets."

To show trends in data such as annual revenues, bar and line charts are useful. For example, by using a bar or line chart, it is easy to see the declining trend in revenue.

The point here is that the more graphical the presentation is, the more likely the audience is to understand your point. After all, a picture is worth a thousand words—or numbers.

Conclusion

Financial reporting plays an important role in any nonprofit organization. In fact, the entire accounting and budgeting process is ultimately centered on producing financial reports. However, producing financial statements is only the beginning. In order to be of value, financial statements must be analyzed and reported to management who can make strategic decisions based on the information.

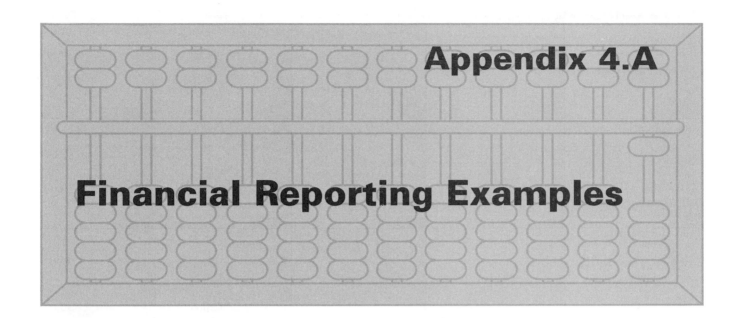

Appendix 4.A

Financial Reporting Examples

ABC Welfare Organization
Statement of Financial Position
December 31, 2002 and 2001

Assets	2002	2001
Current assets		
Cash and cash equivalents	800,000	1,000,000
Other investments	115,000	125,000
Pledges receivable	65,000	45,000
Accounts receivable	10,000	5,000
Other assets	50,000	35,000
Prepaids	30,000	20,000
Total current assets	1,070,000	1,230,000
Property, land, and equipment		
Land and building	1,500,000	1,500,000
Furniture and equipment	500,000	495,000
Vehicles	70,000	60,000
Less: accumulated depreciation	(600,000)	(585,000)
Total property, land, and equipment	1,470,000	1,470,000
Temporarily restricted assets		
Cash	7,000	7,000
Investments	70,000	70,000
Total temporarily restricted assets	77,000	77,000
Permanently restricted assets		
Cash	97,000	97,000
Investments	26,000	26,000
Total permanently restricted assets	123,000	123,000
Total assets	**2,740,000**	**2,900,000**

Liabilities and Net Assets	2002	2001
Liabilities		
Accounts payable and accrued expenses	10,000	15,000
Accrued expenses	38,000	25,000
Notes payable	300,000	310,000
Total liabilities	**348,000**	**350,000**
Net assets		
Undesignated	192,000	350,000
Board-designated reserve	2,000,000	2,000,000
	-	-
Total unrestricted	2,192,000	2,350,000
Temporarily restricted	77,000	77,000
Permanently restricted	123,000	123,000
Total net assets	**2,392,000**	**2,550,000**
Total liabilities and net assets	**2,740,000**	**2,900,000**

ABC Welfare Organization

Statement of Program Expenses

Summary of Total Operations for the 6 Months Ending December 31, 2002

	Current Month				Year to Date				
	Prior-Year Actual	Actual	Budget	Variance	Prior-Year Actual	Actual	Budget	Variance	Annual Budget
Salaries and wages	83,300	114,300	116,000	(1,700)	462,000	579,000	584,000	(5,000)	1,168,000
Fringe benefits	24,800	23,000	40,000	(17,000)	93,000	127,000	166,800	(39,800)	333,600
Stipends, volunteer help	400	6,700	7,000	(300)	40,200	23,800	42,000	(18,200)	84,000
Consultants and professional fee	9,700		2,000	(2,000)	21,100	9,700	12,000	(2,300)	24,000
Licenses and permits	500		1,000	(1,000)	1,000	200	6,000	(5,800)	12,000
Contract or casual labor	800	300	1,300	(1,000)	3,000	2,300	7,800	(5,500)	15,600
Accounting and auditing	10,600	8,600	9,800	(1,200)	76,500	10,600	12,000	(1,400)	24,000
Computer consulting		8,400	8,000	400	5,100	5,100	10,000	(4,900)	20,000
Payroll processing fee	300	300	500	(200)	1,100	800	3,000	(2,200)	6,000
Social work consulting		300	500	(200)	100	1,200	3,000	(1,800)	6,000
Other consulting services	100		100	(100)	10,300	100	600	(500)	1,200
Travel and transportation	400	600	600	0	1,700	2,700	3,600	(900)	7,200
Equipment and supplies	2,100	6,400	2,800	3,600	15,600	25,000	16,800	8,200	33,600
Medications	5,000	600	6,400	(5,800)	26,600	7,000	10,000	(3,000)	20,000
Medical supplies and lab fees	2,700	2,000	3,000	(1,000)	22,100	8,500	10,000	(1,500)	20,000
Food purchases	16,000	24,000	21,000	3,000	138,900	141,000	131,800	9,200	263,600
Purchases clothing		300	300	0	300	1,000	1,800	(800)	3,600
Supplies for meetings and other programs	1,300		200	(200)	500	400	1,200	(800)	2,400
Printing and copying	1,300	1,000	1,800	(800)	8,000	12,600	10,800	1,800	21,600
Telephone and faxes	1,300	3,600	1,600	2,000	8,300	15,400	9,600	5,800	19,200
Postage and delivery	400	400	600	(200)	3,800	6,800	3,600	3,200	7,200
Rent, food storage	200	3,300	200	3,100	3,900	9,200	1,200	8,000	2,400
Equipment rental	300	200	500	(300)	600	1,200	3,000	(1,800)	6,000
Reimbursements			100	(100)	100	100	600	(500)	1,200
Utilities	1,000	2,000	1,400	600	7,300	16,300	8,400	7,900	16,800
Vehicle, repair and maintenance	100	100	100	0	4,800	1,900	600	1,300	1,200
Vehicle, gas	400	400	700	(300)	3,600	2,700	4,200	(1,500)	8,400
Equipment repair and maintenance		400	400	0	600	2,800	2,400	400	4,800
Building repair and maintenance	700	2,000	600	1,400	8,300	7,800	3,600	4,200	7,200

	Current Month				Year to Date				Annual Budget
	Prior-Year Actual	Actual	Budget	Variance	Prior-Year Actual	Actual	Budget	Variance	
Security	100	1,400	100	1,300	700	1,700	600	1,100	1,200
Cleaning, trash removal, and pest control	700	3,000	900	2,100	4,200	11,000	5,400	5,600	10,800
Evaluation			300	(300)	400		1,800	(1,800)	3,600
Client emergency fund	4,700	1,800	7,000	(5,200)	7,800	6,200	7,000	(800)	14,000
Insurance			2,000	(2,000)	19,000	100	200	(100)	400
Penalties and fines		100	100	0	100	200	600	(400)	1,200
Volunteer corps and internships	100		100	(100)	8,800	5,000	600	4,400	1,200
Bank service charges	700	1,000	800	200	3,600	2,100	4,800	(2,700)	9,600
Newsletter		7,000	7,000	0	13,700	11,300	7,000	4,300	14,000
Advertising and promotion			27,000	(27,000)	22,700	200	500	(300)	1,000
Dues and subscriptions	1,000	1,400	2,000	(600)	1,900	4,400	5,000	(600)	10,000
Special events		200	500	(300)	5,900	900	1,500	(600)	3,000
Donor appeals	20,000	50,700	26,700	24,000	148,100	50,700	55,000	(4,300)	110,000
Other fund-raising		2,200	2,500	(300)		2,100	10,000	(7,900)	20,000
United Way/CFC campaign		1,800	2,000	(200)		1,800	4,000	(2,200)	8,000
Community development	1,700		1,300	(1,300)	1,800	4,600	7,800	(3,200)	15,600
Interest expense			8,800	(8,800)		1,200	8,800	(7,600)	17,600
Property taxes			2,200	(2,200)		1,400	2,000	(600)	4,000
Depreciation	6,300	7,300	7,300	0	37,700	30,000	35,000	(5,000)	70,000
Miscellaneous expenses	200	300	1,000	(700)	1,100	2,000	2,000	0	4,000
Uncategorized expenses				0	100	1,000	0	1,000	
In-kind expenses	117,300	77,000	127,900	(50,900)	475,000	415,000	385,000	30,000	770,000
G&A allocation									
Total expenses	315,200	364,400	456,000	(91,600)	1,721,000	1,575,100	1,615,000	(39,900)	3,230,000

ABC Welfare Organization

Statement of Program Expenses

Food Program for the 6 Months Ending December 31, 2002

	Current Month				Year to Date				Annual Budget
	Prior-Year Actual	Actual	Budget	Variance	Prior-Year Actual	Actual	Budget	Variance	
Salaries and wages	12,900	15,000	14,000	1,000	70,000	90,000	84,000	6,000	168,000
Fringe benefits	3,700	2,500	2,500	0	14,300	22,200	15,000	7,200	30,000
Stipends, volunteer help	400	3,000	2,200	800	1,000	18,000	13,200	4,800	26,400
Licenses and permits		100	100	0		200	600	(400)	1,200
Contract or casual labor	600	700	800	(100)	1,200	2,100	4,800	(2,700)	9,600
Travel and transportation		600	500	100		700	3,000	(2,300)	6,000
Equipment and supplies	200	1,000	1,000	0	1,400	2,300	6,000	(3,700)	12,000
Food purchases	16,000	24,000	21,000	3,000	138,900	141,000	131,800	9,200	263,600
Supplies for meetings and other programs		800	1,000	(200)	100	1,000	6,000	(5,000)	12,000
Printing and copying	300	200	300	(100)	1,500	2,500	1,800	700	3,600
Telephone and faxes	2,500	700	300	400	1,500	3,000	1,800	1,200	3,600
Postage and delivery	100	100	100	0	800	1,500	600	900	1,200
Rent, food storage	200	3,300	200	3,100	3,900	8,800	1,200	7,600	2,400
Equipment rental	300	500	500	0	300	1,100	3,000	(1,900)	6,000
Vehicle, repair and maintenance		500	500	0	3,600	1,300	3,000	(1,700)	6,000
Vehicle, gas		200	700	(500)	2,400	1,300	4,200	(2,900)	8,400
In-kind expenses	20,100	20,000	18,000	2,000	142,900	144,000	145,000	(1,000)	290,000
G&A allocation	5,800	6,500	7,000	(500)	29,100	34,000	42,000	(8,000)	84,000
Total expenses	63,100	79,700	70,700	9,000	412,900	475,000	467,000	8,000	934,000

ABC Welfare Organization

Statement of Activities for the 6 Months Ending December 31, 2002

	Current Month				Prior-Year Actual	Year to Date			Annual Budget
	Prior-Year Actual	Actual	Budget	Variance		Actual	Budget	Variance	
Support and revenues for operations									
Contributions, individuals	250,000	253,000	263,000	(10,000)	424,000	413,700	439,100	(25,400)	878,200
Contributions, religious groups	22,000	4,200	41,000	(36,800)	35,000	16,300	61,500	(45,200)	123,000
Contributions, corporations	29,000	5,400	32,000	(26,600)	31,000	13,600	33,700	(20,100)	67,400
Contributions, foundations	68,000	47,300	78,000	(30,700)	131,300	84,600	150,200	(65,600)	300,400
Contributions, other organization	1,000	7,500	2,700	4,800	1,000	8,500	3,500	5,000	7,000
Contributions, federal government			29,600	(29,600)			29,600	(29,600)	59,200
Contributions, local government			5,000	(5,000)		28,000	28,000	0	56,000
Other events revenue	1,000	750	750	0	1,500	7,000	10,000	(3,000)	20,000
Investment income	7,000	2,500	46,500	(44,000)	13,000	5,000	29,800	(24,800)	59,600
Miscellaneous income						100			
Total cash revenues	378,000	320,650	498,550	(177,900)	636,800	576,800	785,400	(208,700)	1,570,800
In-kind support									
Food	20,600	21,500	23,000	(1,500)	143,700	154,100	162,000	(7,900)	324,000
Clothing	22,200	21,000	32,000	(11,000)	127,400	82,000	185,000	(103,000)	370,000
Medications	33,500	2,900	25,000	(22,100)	166,600	19,000	226,000	(207,000)	452,000
Legal services	15,100	10,600	20,000	(9,400)	58,500	59,400	75,000	(15,600)	150,000
Medical services	25,000	21,000	26,300	(5,300)	194,000	151,000	204,000	(53,000)	408,000
Total in-kind support	116,400	77,000	126,300	(49,300)	690,200	465,500	852,000	(386,500)	1,704,000
Total revenue	494,400	397,650	624,850	(227,200)	1,327,000	1,042,300	1,637,400	(595,200)	3,274,800
Expenses									
Program services									
Food program	63,100	79,700	70,700	9,000	412,900	475,000	467,000	8,000	934,000

	Current Month				Year to Date				Annual
	Prior-Year Actual	Actual	Budget	Variance	Prior-Year Actual	Actual	Budget	Variance	Budget
Clothing program	30,400	29,500	45,500	(16,000)	173,600	137,200	140,000	(2,800)	280,000
Medical program	88,300	48,200	113,000	(64,800)	501,500	308,000	325,000	(17,000)	650,000
Legal services	46,700	56,000	69,800	(13,800)	206,300	308,400	334,000	(25,600)	668,000
Total program services	228,500	213,400	299,000	(85,600)	1,294,300	1,228,600	1,266,000	(37,400)	2,532,000
Supporting services									
Fund-raising	80,000	130,000	132,000	(2,000)	326,700	249,500	251,000	(1,500)	502,000
General and administrative	6,700	21,000	25,000	(4,000)	100,000	97,000	98,000	(1,000)	196,000
Total supporting services	86,700	151,000	157,000	(6,000)	426,700	346,500	349,000	(2,500)	698,000
Total expenses	315,200	364,400	456,000	(91,600)	1,721,000	1,575,100	1,615,000	(39,900)	3,230,000
Net revenue (expense)	179,200	33,250	168,850	(135,600)	(394,000)	(532,800)	22,400	(555,300)	44,800

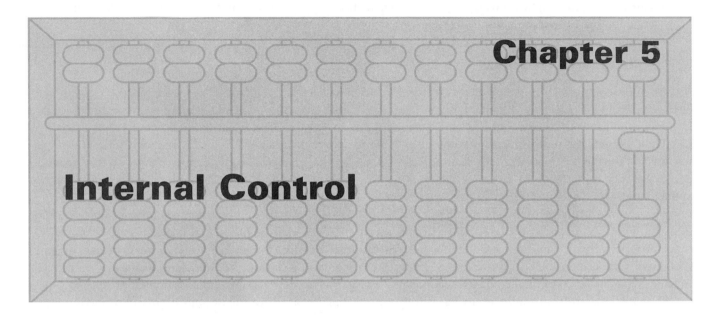

Chapter 5

Internal Control

Associations and not-for-profit organizations (collectively, the "associations") by their nature do not have owners, and do not exist to generate income for these owners. These organizations exist to accomplish a specific purpose, and they expend their resources accordingly. The organization's resources are normally provided by individuals or groups with an interest in the organization's purpose, such as members, donors, or the government. The association is held accountable to these providers for how it expends its resources. Protecting these resources and properly reporting their use are of critical importance to associations.

In a typical association, responsibility for the safeguarding of assets and accuracy of financial reporting is distributed among different levels of the organization: the board of directors, the treasurer, a budget or finance committee, an audit committee, the chief financial officer (CFO), and the accounting department.

Overview of the Association Structure

The board of directors is responsible for overseeing the association's accounting and financial reporting policies and procedures. The board is typically elected by the membership, in some fashion, and must answer to the members. These governance positions are normally held by volunteers serving limited terms. Specific roles are often delegated by the board to the officers of the organization and to various committees that assist the board in fulfilling its fiduciary duties.

The treasurer is responsible for all fiscal matters of the association. He or she is usually the liaison between the CFO and the board, presents the financial statements to the board, and proposes financial policies to the board for final approval. The treasurer normally sits on a committee made up of other board members, which is tasked with establishing and monitoring compliance with the financial policies of the organization. This committee is often called the budget or finance committee. The budget or finance committee generally has specific responsibility for making recommendations to the whole board on the organization's budget, capital expenditures, financing, and other significant financial transactions.

The audit committee serves as the link between the board and its outside auditors. These committees are designed to oversee and monitor the financial reporting process and coordinate the effort of the independent auditors. Specific responsibilities of the audit committee often include the following:

- Selecting the independent auditors
- Reviewing the timing and scope of the audit with the auditors
- Reviewing the audit results and audit report with the auditors
- Reviewing the management letter issued by the auditor and ensuring follow up action is taken as appropriate

- Considering the implications of any disagreements between the auditor and management or difficulties encountered during the audit
- Monitoring the relationship between management and the auditor to ensure no risk to the auditor's independence exists

An audit committee generally consists of three to five members of the board. Committee members ideally will have a working knowledge of financial reports, good business practices, and GAAP for nonprofit organizations. In many organizations, the budget or finance committee also serves as the de facto audit committee.

The CFO sets the tone and enforces the policies for the entire organization. This individual is ultimately responsible for the completeness and accuracy of the financial statements. The CFO should have the background and experience to perform the duties of this position effectively. This would generally include education in finance and accounting as well as knowledge and training in GAAP and tax issues of nonprofit organizations.

The size and structure of the accounting department varies with the size and financial resources of the organization as a whole. A controller typically supervises the preparation and analysis of internal financial statements, monitors actual performance against the budget, handles investments, and files tax returns. Accounting managers or staff accountants are responsible for reconciling accounts, preparing journal entries, and producing financial statements. Accounting assistants typically handle transaction processing, such as cash receipts input or invoice processing.

Each of these groups or individuals has a role in protecting the assets of the organization and properly reporting their use. The means by which these objectives are accomplished is referred to as internal control.

Definition of Internal Control

The American Institute of Certified Public Accountants in Statement of Auditing Standard No. 78, "Consideration of Internal Controls in a Financial Statement Audit" defines *internal control* as "a process—effected by an entity's board of directors, management, and other personnel—designed to provide reasonable assurance regarding the achievement of objectives in the following categories: (a) reliability of financial reporting, (b) effectiveness and efficiency of operations, and (c) compliance with applicable laws and regulations." The standard states that internal control consists of five components:

- Control environment
- Risk assessment
- Control activities
- Information and communication
- Monitoring

The Components of Internal Control

Control Environment

The control environment is the foundation on which the four other components stand. An effective control environment sends the message to all involved with the organization that the responsibilities for protection of the organization's assets and proper financial reporting are taken seriously. Many factors influence the control environment. Management's attitude sets the tone. Management should demonstrate integrity in its interaction with employees, members, vendors, customers, and others at all times. They should expect employees to exhibit the same integrity. Management should establish hiring practices to ensure that employees are honest and capable. Background and reference checks should be performed on candidates considered for accounting positions. Once hired, these employees should be trained for their duties. Regular vacations should be required, and duties should be rotated while vacation is taken.

The board should establish a written code of conduct. Example provisions of such a code would include

- Prohibition (or disclosure) of significant financial interests in customers or vendors
- Prohibition (or disclosure) of gifts or special privileges from customers or vendors
- Prohibition of bribes, kickbacks, or other forms of compensation to induce favorable contract terms

Employees should be required to sign declarations of their compliance with conflict-of-interest policies on an annual basis.

The board and its committees play an important role in the control environment of a nonprofit organization. The bylaws of the organization normally describe the duties and responsibilities of the board of directors and committees. These bylaws should be reviewed regularly and updated as necessary to ensure that the role of these groups is clearly defined. Members of the board should be independent of management to ensure proper oversight. Directors should meet in regularly scheduled meetings and keep clear, complete minutes. The board should be provided with financial reports sufficiently detailed to keep them informed of the financial affairs of the organization. The board or its committees should be involved in significant organizational decisions, such as compensation of executives, investment policies, and appointment of auditors. They should be made aware of sensitive issues or items of exposure and follow up as necessary. Without an effective control environment, the other components of internal control cannot be implemented successfully.

Risk Assessment

The risk assessment component of internal control is how management identifies risks to their goals of safeguarding assets and proper financial reporting and how they manage these risks. Management should look at the processing of transactions in the organization, identify where misstatements could occur, and establish controls to prevent or promptly detect those misstatements. The independent auditors perform a risk assessment every year. They may have checklists that the management could use to assess the organization's controls on an ongoing basis. Each time a change is introduced into the organization, management must consider how its policies, processes, and controls may be affected and determine what action, if any, must be taken to ensure its goals are not compromised. Some examples of changes that should be evaluated are

- Changes in the operating environment
- New or temporary personnel
- New or upgraded information systems and technology
- Expansion or growth in programs or funding sources
- New accounting pronouncements or laws and regulations

The key to successful risk assessment is identifying the risks as early as possible. Management should be proactive when considering any changes to ensure the full impact is evaluated and the control activities can be modified as appropriate. With respect to new accounting pronouncements, laws, and regulations, management should subscribe to industry alerts and maintain contact throughout the year with outside advisors and auditors to ensure that any necessary modifications in policies and procedures can be made.

Control Activities

Control activities are the mechanisms used by management to ensure that its instructions are followed. They encompass all policies and procedures implemented to achieve the organization's goals. Control activities tend to include the following:

- Performance reviews
- Processing controls
- Physical controls
- Segregation of duties

Performance Reviews

Comparison of operating results to the budget, to forecasts, and to prior-year results are effective methods for analyzing the accuracy of financial reporting. The annual budgeting process is one of the best methods to establish financial controls in an organization. Most organizations establish an operating budget and a capital budget for acquiring fixed assets. An effective budget process provides a framework for planning the activities of the organization, measuring its performance, and controlling costs. A budget process that includes steps for providing proper guidance and instruction, involving appropriate levels of management and requiring board approval will result in a budget that is a meaningful control mechanism. Of course, the budget will be useless if the accounting system cannot produce reports that compare actual results to the budget on a timely basis. Financial reports should be produced monthly, with variances from the budget highlighted and explained. Unusual results should be investigated by the CFO and reported to senior management and the board.

Processing Controls

Processing controls are the activities that ensure that each transaction is initiated, processed, and recorded accurately. Procedures should be established to ensure that no transactions are omitted from the records. Likewise, steps should exist to ensure that no fictitious or duplicate transactions are recorded. Controls should be implemented to ensure that transactions are recorded in the proper account, amount, and period. The following are examples of processing controls:

- Department supervisors review and initial timesheets before submitting them to the accounting department.
- The CFO reviews and approves the accounts payable voucher prior to signing checks.
- Bank-stamped deposit tickets are compared to the daily receipt log and posted to the cash receipts journal.

Physical Controls

Physical controls involve the physical security of the organization's tangible assets and records. Physical controls include access to computer programs and data files. Most associations depend heavily on computers in their financial reporting systems, and it is imperative that computer controls also be established as part of the overall system of internal control. Controls should be implemented over the acquisition, development, and maintenance of application systems and over the use of and change to data maintained on computer files. Measures should be taken to back up data routinely and store backup information off-site. A disaster recovery plan should be formulated.

Segregation of Duties

One of the most important concepts of internal control is segregation of duties. It is important that in any accounting process no one individual have the ability to authorize the transaction, record the transaction, maintain custody of the related asset, if applicable, and perform the control designed to prevent or detect errors in the transaction. Neglecting to separate the responsibility for these functions provides an opportunity for errors to go undetected, and for an individual to misappropriate assets and hide what they did. The importance of this concept will be illustrated as we discuss specific control procedures in typical applications.

Applying Control Procedures

Cash Receipts

In establishing controls over cash receipts, it is important to identify all sources of those receipts—that is, revenue sources (such as dues payments, meeting registrations, or exhibitor rental fees), proceeds from the sale of fixed assets or investments, or bank borrowings—so controls over each source can be implemented. It is also important to identify the form of the receipts—that is, currency, check, credit card payments, or wire transfers—because they each have a different risk for misappropriation.

Establishing appropriate authority is particularly relevant in the cash receipts area. The board should authorize the opening and closing of all bank accounts and determine who will have responsibility for making deposits or authorizing wire transfers. Additionally, all employees handling cash should be covered by a fidelity bond. A fidelity bond is insurance purchased by the organization to cover losses because of employee theft or dishonesty. Access to cash receipts and the related accounting records should be provided to only those authorized.

If the volume of cash receipts is high, such as is often the case with membership dues, the organization should consider a lockbox arrangement. With a lockbox, the organization sends preaddressed envelopes with its invoices and asks that members use the envelopes to return payments. The address is a post office box at the bank. The money is deposited immediately into the organization's account, and all supporting documents are sent to the organization for processing. The benefit to the lockbox is that money is available immediately, improving cash flow, and employees never have access to the cash, reducing opportunity for misappropriation.

Checks coming into the office directly should also be subject to controls. Ideally, two individuals will be present when mail is opened. A listing of all checks should be prepared, and the checks should be immediately restrictively endorsed. The "for deposit only" endorsement should include the full name of the organization and the bank account number. The checks should be given to another individual to make the deposit to the bank, and still another should be responsible for recording the deposit. Finally, another individual should compare the original listing of checks to the deposit slip and the amount recorded.

Many associations encounter situations in which checks are given to employees in other departments instead of sending the funds by mail. For instance, a corporate sponsor may give their check to the meetings director at the meeting. One goal of internal control over cash receipts is to make a record of the receipt as soon as it is received. Management must communicate the importance of this to all employees and establish policies and procedures to ensure that such hand-delivered checks go to the proper employees to deposit and that receipts are recorded as soon as possible.

Associations often have conventions or educational meetings that are a significant source of revenue. The majority of this revenue often comes in advance from attendees or exhibitors, but there are often on-site transactions that must be controlled. A reconciliation should be performed daily of the cash received at the meeting to the supporting documents (registration forms, tickets sold, etc.) If a "store" is set up to sell merchandise or publications, cash registers should be utilized to record the sales. Cashiers should be supervised, and the register tape reconciled to the cash at the end of each day. Some retailers will put signs on the register offering free merchandise if the cashier does not give the customer his receipt. This is done to ensure that the register is used to capture every transaction, because a customer receipt is not possible unless the register is used.

Regardless of the source, all cash receipts should be deposited intact daily. If this is not possible, the receipts should be locked in a safe with access restricted to authorized personnel.

Cash Disbursements

Similar to the cash receipts processing, it is important to identify the activities that give rise to disbursements (i.e., payments for routine operating expenses, capital expenditures, expense reimbursements, debt repayments, investing activities) and the form of disbursements used by the organization (currency, check, wire). This analysis must be performed to determine where controls need to be implemented to prevent loss of funds.

As with cash receipts, assigning appropriate authority for the approval of disbursements and signing of checks is critical. Segregation of duties is essential in the disbursement of cash function. The individual preparing checks and maintaining the check register should not have the authority to sign checks and approve invoices for payment. Someone else should also mail the checks. Policies are crucial to establishing the proper control environment in the cash disbursements area. Payments should be made on original invoices only, not on vendor statements. Check signers should be approved by the board, and any changes communicated to the bank immediately. Two signatures should be required on checks over a certain dollar amount, again, with the threshold set by the board. Checks should not be signed unless the supporting documents have been reviewed and initialed by an authorized individual. Supporting documents should be marked "PAID" or otherwise canceled to prevent reuse.

Steps should be taken to protect blank checks, signature plates, and check-signing machines when they are used. Specifically, blank checks should be locked up at all times, and access to the checks should be limited to the person authorized to prepare them. Checks should be prenumbered and used in sequence. Some banks now provide encoding software that applies the routing and other bank information directly to the check as it is printed. In this way, blank check stock is worthless. Access to signature plates and check-signing machines should also be limited, preferably to one individual, and should be kept in a locked file or safe when not in use. A log of the checks (by number) signed by the machine should be kept and monitored by the individual approving the supporting documentation.

The controls discussed previously involve controls over payments made by check. Similar controls should be established for other forms of payments. Authorization for wire transfers should be delegated appropriately.

Organizations can set up their accounts so that wires can only go to preset accounts, such as other accounts held by the organization or a lender.

Payroll

The payroll process is a special area of disbursements and requires unique controls. Payroll and the related benefits are often the largest expense for nonprofit organizations. Controls should be in place to ensure that all obligations for compensable work performed by employees are recorded when incurred. Similarly, controls should prevent fictitious or duplicate obligations from being recorded and should help ensure that payments are made in the proper amounts, are recorded to the proper account, and are reflected in the proper period.

The number of employees, the number of offices, and the nature of the workforce (salary versus hourly) can impact the level of controls that should be implemented. Segregation of duties is again critical to the success of the controls. Ideally, the individual responsible for approving salaries, hiring additional employees, and terminating personnel would review the payroll and sign checks but would not be responsible for maintaining payroll records or preparing the checks. Similarly, another independent individual would be responsible for distributing the checks.

Many associations outsource the payroll function to service organizations that specialize in processing payroll, calculating related tax withholdings and liabilities, and remitting required taxes. This is an excellent option to ensure compliance with tax regulations, but it does not alleviate the organization's obligation for reviewing the reports generated and payments made by the payroll service.

Regardless of whether payroll is processed in-house, authority for hiring, promoting, and terminating employees and changing salaries should be held at the proper level. If timesheets are used, they should be signed by the employee and his or her supervisor. The individual who prepares the payroll should review the approved timesheets prior to processing. The payroll register should be reviewed by an independent party to ensure that pay rates, hours, total gross pay, and withholdings are reasonable and that no fictitious employees are listed. The amounts for salaries and benefits recorded in the general ledger should be reconciled quarterly with payroll information reported to the Internal Revenue Service.

Additional Controls

There are two additional controls that should be present in all organizations. The first is timely bank reconciliations by a party independent of the authorization, custody, and record-keeping functions. Canceled checks should be compared to the accounting records to verify agreement with dates and payees and should be examined for proper endorsements and cancellations. All reconciling items on the bank reconciliation should be followed up and resolved immediately. These reconciliations should be performed monthly as soon as the bank statement is received. All checks in the sequence should be accounted for. All charges on the bank statement should be recorded. The bank reconciliation should be reviewed by a responsible official.

Another very important control is the timely preparation of monthly financial reports that includes a comparison of actual revenue and expenditures to budget. These statements should be provided to all department heads with budget responsibility, the executive director, and the treasurer. Timely review and oversight can help detect problems such as unauthorized disbursements or missing revenue.

Bank reconciliations and review of monthly statements are forms of controls designed to detect errors or misappropriation after the fact. There are some innovative solutions to help prevent errors too. One is called positive pay. Under this system the organization transmits a data file to the bank listing what checks have been issued. The bank will only pay on checks that have been preapproved. This system can be expensive and administratively cumbersome (especially if the financial institution used does not have a strong system in place), but it is highly successful in identifying unauthorized checks. Some prevention controls can be built right into the disbursement software. For instance, the system may not allow the same vendor invoice number to be entered twice, to help prevent duplicate payments.

The advent of online banking increases efficiencies and offers opportunities for timely monitoring. It can also increase the opportunity for unauthorized expenditures. Only those individuals with check-signing authority should be able to approve payment to vendors by automatic debit.

Information and Communication

With respect to financial reporting, the information system of an organization consists of the procedures and records used to initiate, process, and record transactions and to maintain accountability for the related assets, liabilities, and net assets. Management relies on information generated by the accounting system to make business decisions. The accuracy of this information is therefore critical, and the effective design of this system is imperative to internal control. Examples of questions to ask in considering the design of the system over subscription revenue might be as follows:

- How do we ensure that all valid subscription orders are identified and recorded?
- Does the subscription order form provide sufficient information to ensure that the order is recorded for the proper periodical, for the proper amount, and that the revenue is recorded in the proper period?
- How do we ensure that data from the order entry system gets posted properly to the general ledger?

A similar analysis should be performed for all transaction cycles. The answers to these questions are the control activities that should be implemented.

Communication consists of providing an understanding to individuals in the organization of their roles and responsibilities with respect to internal controls over financial reporting. This is most effectively done by creating and distributing policy and procedures manuals. A standard outline for an accounting policies and procedures manual might look like the sample table of contents given at the end of Chapter 2.

Accounting manuals have a way of being created, placed on a shelf, and forgotten. To be effective, the manual must be used as a training tool, serve as a reference manual, and be adhered to. A review of the manual should be performed annually to determine the need for revision. Keep the manual in a loose-leaf format so that changes to selected sections can be made easily.

Monitoring

Monitoring is the practice of revisiting the internal controls to ensure they are operating as intended and continue to be appropriate. Monitoring typically takes place in two forms: ongoing monitoring and separate evaluations. Ongoing monitoring is achieved in management's involvement in the day-to-day activities of the organization. Management's knowledge of what is happening in the industry can assist in identifying financial results that are not consistent with expectations. Late financial reporting can be indicative of breakdowns in the internal control process. The board also plays a role in ongoing monitoring. Boards who meet regularly, have concise agendas, and demand timely financial information help keep the financial reporting process on track. Separate evaluations are specific periodic procedures in place to monitor controls. Examples would be performance evaluations on personnel and annual audits or member satisfaction surveys.

The five components of internal control contribute to the achievement of the goals of reliable financial reporting, effective and efficient operations, and compliance with applicable laws and regulations.

Special Consideration—Fraud

Overview

No association executive wants to hear the name of his or her organization and the word *fraud* used in the same sentence. Reports of fraud against both for-profit and not-for-profit organizations seem to be prevalent in the news today. The American Institute of Certified Public Accountants issued Statement on Auditing Standards No. 99 (SAS 99) "Consideration of Fraud in a Financial Statement Audit" as a guide to auditors in fulfilling their responsibilities for planning and performing audits to obtain reasonable assurance that the financial statements are free from material misstatement, whether due to error or fraud. For purposes of this statement, fraud is defined as "an intentional act that results in a material misstatement in financial statements that are the subject of an audit." To an association executive, of course, fraud is any intentional act that results in the misappropriation of assets or inaccurate financial reporting, regardless of materiality. SAS 99 states that fraud is most likely to occur when the following three conditions are present: incentive (also referred to as motivation), opportunity, and the ability to rationalize the conduct.

Incentive

Various factors could increase the pressure on employees to commit fraud against the organization. Personal situations that give rise to a need for funds, such as gambling debts, speculative investments, divorce, or medical needs, could lead an individual to look for ways to steal cash or other assets from the organization. Dissatisfied employees with a desire to seek revenge against the organization are also motivated to commit fraud. Fraudulent financial reporting can occur if executive compensation is tied to the organization's financial results, or if a significant source of revenue or financing is dependent on financial position.

Opportunity

Opportunity arises when circumstances exist—typically the absence of internal controls or management's ability to override controls—that allow a fraud to be perpetrated and go undetected. If the nonprofit handles large amounts of cash, or inventory and fixed assets consist of items that have a street value, the organization will be more susceptible to fraud. If there is a lack of segregation of duties and inadequate review and supervision, the opportunity increases. An ineffective board cannot protect against an executive who dominates management.

Rationalization

Perpetrators of fraud often rationalize their actions, believing they are entitled to the funds or assets stolen because of some disservice done to them. Management that continually exhibits attitudes or actions that are inconsistent with establishing a strong control environment are setting the organization up for loss due to fraud.

Common Types of Fraud

Cash

As the most liquid of an organization's assets, cash is the most susceptible to theft or other misappropriation. The following are common schemes involving cash:

- Skimming: In this form of fraud, cash is removed from the organization before it is recorded in the records. This is most common with situations in which a large volume of cash is handled with minimal supervision. A crowded off-site meeting bookstore processing cash sales without registers invites the pocketing of cash.
- Voids and under-rings: This type of fraud occurs in retail operations that use cash registers and can be accomplished in many ways. Cashiers could record a sale and then void the transaction but keep the cash, or they could sell merchandise to friends or family at a discount and then give a full cash refund upon return of the merchandise.
- Check fraud: This type of fraud is becoming increasingly popular with the availability of high-quality laser printers, scanners, color copiers, and improvements in desktop publishing—perpetrators can reproduce a check that is indistinguishable from the organization's actual checks and tender them for payment.
- Diversion of cash receipts: This type of fraud can occur when there is a lack of segregation of duties, and the individual opening the mail is responsible for depositing the receipts. By opening unauthorized accounts in the name of the organization, this individual can divert the funds.

Accounts Receivable

- Lapping: This form of fraud involves the misappropriation of cash by an employee and is covered up by applying cash received from another member or customer to the customer account the money was originally stolen from. That shortage is then covered by the next receipt and so on. This scheme can continue until discovered, the money is repaid, or it is buried by a credit to the customer's account and a miscellaneous debit to an expense account.
- Another form of fraud in accounts receivable involves stealing cash collected on previously written-off accounts.

Inventory and Supplies

A common fraud is the misappropriation of inventory and supplies by employees for personal use. This can also include making personal long-distance calls on the organization's account and making personal copies.

Purchasing

- Fictitious invoices: This fraud involves the setup of a fictitious vendor and subsequent payment of invoices to the vendor.
- Duplicate payments: This fraud involves submission by a vendor of the same invoice.
- Conflict of interest: Conflicts of interest arise when an insider (such as a board member or key executive) can direct the organization to do business with a company in which the insider or a relative of the insider has a financial interest.

Payroll and Personal Expenses

- Fictitious employees: In large organizations, or those with many locations, setting up a fictitious employee on the payroll is a means to misappropriate cash.
- Inflated timesheets: Nonexempt employees can submit timesheets reflecting hours they did not work.
- Personal expense reimbursement: This fraud involves the submission of expense reports that include charges for personal expenditures or charges not incurred.

Protecting the Association from Fraud

There are a number of measures an organization can take to prevent and detect fraud. Many of these were discussed in the earlier sections on internal control. An exhibit to SAS 99 provides suggestions to management on antifraud programs and controls. Although geared primarily to public companies, many of the same concepts apply to nonprofits.

Creating a Culture of Honesty and High Ethics

This concept reflects the intent of the control environment component of internal control that was discussed previously. The board and management should not create a situation in which budget pressures lead employees to manipulate the financial results. Management should create a positive workplace environment to avoid situations in which employees feel they must steal to be rewarded for their efforts or to get what they are due. Organizations should provide training and promotion opportunities and attractive compensation and benefit packages when possible. Finally, if incidents of fraud occur, management needs to take immediate, appropriate action to deter future similar incidents.

Evaluate Antifraud Processes and Controls

This concept reflects the intent of the last four components of internal control discussed previously. In evaluating its processes and controls, management should consider not just where errors could occur but also where fraud could occur. For example, in determining the proper controls over payroll processing, ask questions such as "If the controller wanted to increase the amount of his paycheck, could he do it without detection?" If the answer is yes, implement controls to prevent this, such as a review by the CFO of the payroll register each pay period against a list of authorized salaries.

Develop an Appropriate Oversight Process

This concept reflects the intent of the internal control components of control environment and monitoring discussed previously. An oversight process is crucial to effectively preventing and deterring fraud. One concept worth noting is that board and management should provide a mechanism by which employees can report unethical behavior, actual or suspected fraud, or violations of company policy without fear of reprimand or negative repercussions.

Special Consideration—Internal Control for the Small Association

The discussions in previous sections regarding internal controls and fraud deterrence sound great for associations with large accounting departments and significant resources. However, smaller associations do not have the luxury of complete segregation of duties because of the small number of individuals on staff. Strong internal controls are still important for these associations and should not be deemed *impossible*. Some of the controls to focus on are as follows:

- Board oversight: In small organizations the CFO or executive director often has considerable control and authority over the expenditure of funds. In these situations it is crucial for the board to be active and involved in reviewing financial statements and budgets and asking relevant questions on any unusual activity or variances.

- Treasurer involvement: If the treasurer of the organization is local, consideration should be given to requiring his signature on all checks.

- Hiring practices: Background and reference checks are essential steps in attempting to hire honest employees.

- Fidelity bonding: Insure employees handling cash to protect against dishonesty and theft.

- Cash: Unopened bank statements should be sent to the treasurer or local board member to open and to review the contents for propriety before returning to the staff for reconciling. Checks over a certain amount should be countersigned.

- Physical safeguards: Assets subject to misappropriation (small computers, inventory, supplies, blank checks, undeposited checks, etc.) should be kept in restricted areas with access limited.

- Disaster recovery and contingency planning: Off-premises storage is recommended for master files and transaction files sufficient to recreate them in the event of a computer system crash. Contingency plans should be developed for alternative processing in the event of loss of information technology capabilities.

- Annual audit: The organization should have the financial statements audited on an annual basis.

Checklist of Common Controls

Cash Receipts

- Incoming mail should be opened and a listing of cash and checks received should be made under the supervision of a responsible official. This listing should be compared to the actual deposit made to ensure the completeness of the deposit.

- Checks received should be immediately restrictively endorsed.

- Where practical, a bank lockbox should be utilized to receive payments.

- All cash receipts should be deposited daily, if possible. If not possible, ensure that the undeposited receipts are secured.

- On-site cash collections should be received and counted in the presence of two people, both of whom must certify as to the amount received. Cash registers should be used when practical.

Cash Disbursements

- The clerical accuracy of documents supporting disbursements should be checked.

- No checks should be signed in advance (e.g., signing blank checks for future emergency).

- Access to blank checks, signature stamps, or machines should be restricted.

- Checks should be prenumbered and used in sequence. Voided checks should be defaced and retained.

- Checks should not be returned to the preparer after signing. The supporting documents should be marked *PAID*, or otherwise canceled to prevent duplicate payment.

- Checks should not be signed unless an authorized individual has seen and approved the underlying supporting documentation. Duplicate invoices, phony invoices, and unauthorized amounts should never be paid.

No invoices for goods should be paid until shipping documents indicate they were received. The authorized signer should not also maintain custody of cash or have access to the accounting system.

- A policy should be established that identifies authorized signers and the dollar levels for requiring two signatures.
- Debit memos and wire transfers should be adequately controlled by use of passwords or bank callback verifications.

Other Cash Controls

- Any adjustments to the cash account should be reviewed and approved by a responsible person.
- Cash should be held in reputable institutions that provide FDIC insurance. All bank accounts should be authorized by the board. Any unused accounts should be promptly closed.
- Cash accounts should be reconciled to the general ledger in a timely manner. This reconciliation should be performed by an individual who is independent of the cash receipts and disbursements functions. Old outstanding checks should be investigated and resolved.
- Unopened bank statements should be sent to someone unrelated to the accounting process. This individual should review the canceled checks returned for unusual payees or endorsements, or unusual amounts.
- Individuals handling cash should be included in fidelity bond coverage.

Payroll

- All hiring and salary changes should be conducted in accordance with firm policy and approved by the executive director.
- A periodic review of payroll files should be performed to ensure that they are maintained in accordance with company and government policies. Access to these records should be limited, and the information contained therein should be kept confidential.
- Use an outside payroll service to compute payroll and payroll taxes and prepare necessary tax filings. Payroll registers and the general ledger should be reconciled with the gross and net pay amounts based on the payroll tax returns.
- Establish timekeeping documentation policies and procedures to capture time spent by functional programs. No payment should be made unless supported by evidence of the time worked.
- The payroll register should be reviewed by the executive director or another responsible party who is independent of the payroll processing functions. This is done to identify fictitious employees or unusual amounts.
- Accrued vacation should be tracked and reconciled to the general ledger monthly.

Contributions and Revenue and Related Receivables

- Fund-raising activities should be approved by the board.
- Donations should be acknowledged promptly.
- Donors names should be published in journals or newsletters of the organization, with instructions that any omission should be reported to an individual of the organization to follow up.
- Records of all donations should be kept, including any restrictions on the amount donated. Donations of in-kind gifts or donated services should be tracked as well.
- Promises to give must be tracked when the pledge is received.
- Designate specific employees to assure compliance with the terms and conditions of any awards.
- Dues rates, fees, subscription rates, and so forth should be approved by the board and publicly announced or published.
- Policies for revenue recognitions should be established and monitored.
- Reconcile the revenue recorded to expected revenue (i.e., the number of attendees times the registration rate should approximate the registration revenue recorded).

- Receivables should be reconciled to the general ledger monthly.
- Delinquent accounts should be followed up for collection. Any amounts written off or adjusted should be reviewed by a responsible official.

Investments

- An investment committee or the board should establish an investment policy.
- Any outside broker used should be reputable and be held responsible for adhering to the policy.
- Monthly statements should be reviewed for unusual transactions and reconciled to the general ledger. Any investment earnings should be recorded (by the proper net asset class, as applicable).
- The performance of the investment manager should be periodically reviewed.

Association Insurance Issues

Although an entire chapter (or book) could be written on association insurance matters, some of the types of insurances that could be applicable to associations are as follows:

- Association professional liability: This is the nonprofit version of directors and officers liability insurance.
- Crime: This would cover things such as employee dishonesty, depositors forgery, and money and securities fraud.
- Employment practice liability: Although this could be generically covered in the APL policy, it may be necessary to have separate coverage for this litigation-intensive area.
- Property insurance: This could cover real property, personal property, and computers or loss of income due to a covered event
- Commercial general liability: This could cover events such as bodily injury and property damage, personal injury and advertising liability, medical payments, foreign liability, duty to defend, automobile coverage, and workers compensation and would include an umbrella liability.
- Fiduciary liability and employee benefit liability: This would deal with liability for pension plan issues.
- Publisher's liability: A separate policy for this may be necessary if the association has substantial publishing activity—you may need to consider a separate errors and omissions policy as well.
- Convention and meeting cancellation insurance: This would address the loss that would be incurred if a revenue-producing meeting was canceled, because of a hurricane, earthquake, or some other uncontrollable circumstance.
- Special event liability: This could cover special situations that the nonprofit would engage in such as fund-raising activities like walk-a-thons, bike-a-thons, and so forth.

Of course, associations should seek the counsel of expert insurance professionals to address the types and amounts of coverage they need.

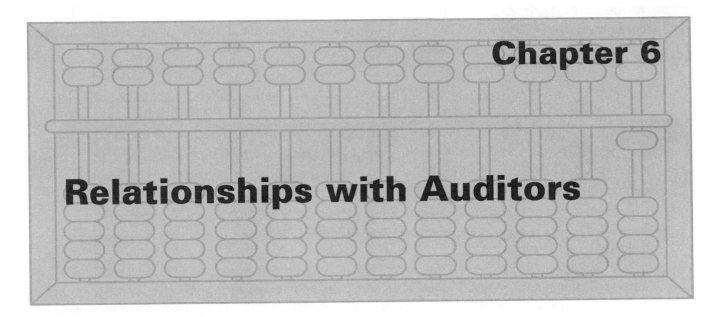

Chapter 6

Relationships with Auditors

Many associations are required to or desire to have their financial statements audited by an independent CPA. Users of financial statements look to the report of the CPA for assurance that the information reported on is relevant and reliable. Contracting for an annual audit is an important responsibility for the board in meeting its fiduciary duty to the organization and, ultimately, the members it represents.

Audit Policy

The organization's accounting policies and procedures manual should include a section on the audit. The policy should include the requirement that the books and records be audited by an independent auditor and indicate how often the audit should be conducted. Procedures should include the steps to follow for selecting the auditor (including how often to go out for bid), evaluating the auditors, and preparing for the audit.

Considerations in Selecting a CPA Firm

There are a number of factors to consider in selecting a CPA firm, among them independence, reputation, experience or expertise, and fees.

Independence

Under the generally accepted auditing standards adopted by the AICPA, CPAs must maintain an independence in mental attitude in all matters relating to an assignment. It is imperative in making a decision about hiring an auditor that the auditor be independent in fact and appearance from the organization he or she is auditing.

Reputation

Another important factor in evaluating CPA firms is the firm's professional reputation. Specific considerations would include the following:

- The firm's size and longevity
- Membership in industry-related professional organizations
- Membership in the AICPA Division of Firms subject to special membership requirements, such as peer review
- Peer review results
- Client reference feedback

Experience or Expertise

An organization needs to evaluate the CPA firm's ability to conduct the audit in an efficient and effective manner. This ability hinges on the firm's experience with organizations of similar size and nature as well as the overall technical capabilities of the staff assigned to the engagement. Consider asking the following questions:

- Does the firm have significant nonprofit industry experience, including audits of organizations of similar size and programs?
- What are the qualifications of the engagement partner and the senior staff assigned to the audit?
- What type of support services (such as newsletters or seminars) does the firm provide?
- What tax, management, and other services can the firm provide without affecting independence?
- If you have multiple locations, does the firm have offices to service these locations?
- If you have for-profit subsidiaries, does the firm have experience outside the nonprofit industry?
- If you have employee benefit plans that require audit, does the firm have experience in these audits?

Fees

Obviously, fees are an important consideration when evaluating professional service providers. Most audit engagements are bid on a fixed-fee basis, with a provision for additional billing if the scope of services to be provided expands or if difficulties are encountered. When evaluating proposals, the organization should ensure that fees for all services to be provided are clearly spelled out. Questions to ask would include

- How are fees determined?
- How are overruns handled when problems are encountered?
- What are the standard billing procedures for accounting consultations throughout the year?
- Are out-of-pocket expenses billed separately?

The Selection Process

As previously mentioned, the accounting policies and procedures manual should include a section on selecting an auditor, periodically reviewing the selection, and preparing for the annual audit. Normally, this will include an outline of the information to be requested in a written request for proposal (RFP). The first step is determining which firms will be sent the request. Organizations should talk to their peers at similar organizations, ask professional organizations or the state society of CPAs, and visit Web sites. A detailed RFP should then be sent to these organizations. See Appendix 6.A at the end of this chapter for an example RFP. It is usually helpful to the audit firms if you include a copy of your audited financial statements from the prior year, any tax returns, and the most recent internal financial statements.

Once proposals are received, they should be compared on the factors that are important to the organization. Often, creating a table summarizing the components of each proposal so that firms can be evaluated side by side will be helpful. Most associations will narrow down the selections to a few firms and schedule meetings with the candidates to discuss their proposal.

The board of the association must decide who will have the ultimate authority to engage the audit firm and will be largely responsible for the effectiveness and success of the relationship. One of the best practices is for the board to designate an audit committee to take responsibility for audit oversight. A charter should be written and implemented to clearly define the audit committee's duties. The charter should include the purpose of the committee, its composition, the frequency of meetings, and the detailed responsibilities of the committee. The charter helps define what the committee's oversight role is and is not, and it can help prevent the committee from micromanaging the organization's staff.

Often, the management of the organization handles the RFP process to the point of narrowing down the choices. These firms should present their proposals to the audit committee. The audit committee should then make the recommendation for the auditor to the full board. It is important for the audit committee to let the auditors know that they are reporting to the committee and not to management. Once the auditor has been chosen, the engagement will move into the planning stage.

The Audit

Planning Stage

During this stage you will contract formally with the audit firm, and the auditors will take steps to understand your operations and your internal control in order to plan their procedures. The chairman of the board of directors or the audit committee should expect to sign an engagement letter, which is essentially a letter that outlines the agreement between the association and the auditor, specifically the responsibilities of management and the auditor and any limitations of the engagement. The auditor will likely schedule interviews to obtain an understanding of your accounting systems and processes. To the extent that documentation already exists describing your governance and accounting structure, you should provide this to the auditors.

After the initial phase, the auditor will normally provide management with a detailed listing of all schedules and supporting documents needed to complete the audit. A sample of such a letter is in Appendix 6.B, at the end of this chapter. Many organizations find that the audit runs more smoothly when the controller coordinates the information exchange between the auditors and the nonprofit staff. The controller should assign each item on the auditor's request list to an accounting or other staff member and review each schedule as it is completed for accuracy. The controller should also record when each item is provided to the auditor. It is in the organization's best interest to have every item on the list ready for the auditor when asked for it. Auditors often make their fee estimates contingent on timely receipt of all requested items. By managing the list, the controller can prevent delays that may result in additional billings. The organization should provide as many of the schedules in electronic format as possible. This not only adds efficiency for the auditor, but it facilitates preparation of the same schedules in subsequent years.

Fieldwork

Fieldwork is the stage at which the auditors are on site conducting their procedures. Most auditors try to respect the schedules of their clients and minimize disruption, but management should realize that their involvement in this stage is critical to the efficiency of the audit. The organization should ensure that the audit is scheduled when financial personnel and program management will be available to answer questions and pull supporting documentation. In the planning phase, the auditor determines the extent, nature, and timing of procedures to be performed. In some circumstances they may determine that it is more efficient and effective to perform certain procedures at an interim date, that is, 1 or 2 months prior to year-end, instead of waiting until after year-end. Some common interim procedures are tests of controls, accounts-receivable confirmations, or tests of meeting or event revenue and expenses when the event has already occurred. Performing procedures at an interim date has the added benefit of reducing the audit steps needed at year-end and speeding up the delivery of final statements.

Wrap Up

Once the auditors have completed their on site work, the audit moves into the wrap up phase. At this time management should expect to see draft financial statements, tax returns, and management letters. Management letters are the tools auditors use to communicate with management and the board about their audit findings. These often include the following:

- Deficiencies in internal control
- Suggestions for changing systems, policies, or procedures to improve operating efficiency
- Suggestions relating to accounting matters discovered during the audit
- Communication of new or pending accounting or tax matters that may impact the client

One of the final steps prior to issuance of the financial statements is the signing of the representation letter. The CPA is required to obtain written representation from the client on a number of matters. The management personnel requested to sign the letter should read the letter thoroughly to ensure that they fully understand each item. If there are any events, transactions, or circumstances that would change the representations as written, they should be brought immediately to the auditor's attention. Similarly, if there are negative representations listed (e.g., "We are not aware of any. . . .") that you know have been disclosed, ask to modify the statement to read "except as disclosed to you during the course of the audit." See an example representation letter at Appendix 6.C.

The auditors are required to communicate certain matters to the audit committee (or equivalent) at the conclusion of the audit. These are as follows:

- The auditor's responsibility under generally accepted auditing standards, specifically that the audit is designed to obtain reasonable, rather than absolute, assurance about the financial statements
- The initial selection of and changes to significant accounting policies or their application
- The process used by management in developing sensitive accounting estimates, and the auditor's opinion on the reasonableness of those estimates
- Audit adjustments proposed, both posted and unrecorded
- The auditor's responsibility for other information included in documents including audited financial statements
- Disagreements with management
- The results of consultations with other accountants.
- Major issues discussed with management prior to retention
- Difficulties encountered in performing the audit

At the end of the audit, the management and accounting staff should evaluate the performance of the auditing firm and submit their comments and concerns to the audit committee. This will include a review of the following areas:

1. What was the overall quality of the services provided?
   - Did the auditor's exhibit an understanding of the organization's business?
   - Did engagement seniors and executive-level personnel understand the nonprofit industry?
   - Was the audit staff properly supervised and trained?
2. Were the auditors responsive to requests for assistance?
   - Do auditors return phone calls and e-mails in a timely manner?
   - Do the auditors provide practical solutions to issues?
3. Were deadlines met?
   - Did fieldwork begin and end in accordance with the agreed-upon schedule?
   - Were draft financial statements delivered when promised?
   - Were management letters delivered with the draft financial statements?
   - Were final reports issued when promised?
4. Were management letters appropriate?
5. Were the auditors efficient?
   - Were the auditors organized to prevent loss of schedules and duplicate requests?
   - Was the disruption to your staff minimal?
   - Was there timely executive-level review of the work?
6. Did the audit partner devote sufficient time to the engagement?
7. Were fees in line with the engagement letter?

The audit committee should not hesitate to make suggestions to the auditor for improving the process in the next year.

The audit is an excellent tool for associations to meet their constituents' need for reliable financial information, and in many ways it serves as a deterrent for employee or management dishonesty.

Appendix 6.A

Sample Request for Proposal

XYZ association

March 30, 20XX

Mr. Partner
CPA Firm
1234 Accounting Lane
Anytown, USA

Dear Mr. Partner:

The XYZ Association (XYZ) is seeking proposals from selected certified public accounting firms that have extensive experience in providing audit and tax services to not-for-profit associations.

XYZ is a Section 501(c)(6) not-for-profit professional association representing over 150,000 members. XYZ's budgeted operating revenue for 20XX is $50 million, plus an additional $2 million in grant funds. Membership dues represent approximately 52% of XYZ's revenue. Non-dues revenue sources include investment income, an annual convention, subscription revenue, and advertising in our publications. The advertising revenue is considered unrelated business income and is subject to federal and state income taxes. XYZ staff consists of approximately 250 employees at its Anytown location.

XYZ is requesting a 3-year bid from your firm for the performance of services, as described on the enclosed outline. The prices quoted should be not-to-exceed amounts that would include all incidental expenses.

XYZ has an effective computerized accounting system and an accounting staff willing and able to provide all necessary assistance to the fullest extent allowable in the completion of the audit.

Five copies of your proposals are due by April 30, 20XX, in the format described in the attached document. No proposals received after this date will be considered. Please address your proposal to Mr. CFO at the address on the letterhead.

Enclosed is a copy of XYZ's audited financial statements and Forms 990 and 990-T from the prior year. Please do not hesitate to call if you have any questions.

Sincerely,

Mr. CFO

Enclosures (5)

Minimum Proposal Requirements

Please provide your firm's responses to the following in an executive summary of no more than five pages. Separate supporting schedules should be provided with biographical information, client references, and information about the firm and firm capabilities. Also include the following information:

- Describe what makes your firm uniquely qualified to provide the professional services XYZ requires.
- Include a general discussion of your firm's approach to performing an audit, and the benefits that accrue to XYZ as a result.
- Address the following staffing issues:
  - Provide information about the size and mix of your staff in the office that would be responsible for XYZ's audit.
  - Identify the engagement team who will be performing the work, including their experience and qualifications.
  - Explain how your firm would provide for continuity of staffing on XYZ's audit.
  - Provide demographic information on your personnel, both professional staff and the total staff.
- Address the following work plan issues:
  - Indicate the expected timing and completion of the audit. State how soon after the completion of the fieldwork that we can expect delivery of the draft financial statements and management letters.
  - Include the number of hours expected to be spent by each level of staff and the approximate rate per hour charged.
  - Indicate ways you would utilize XYZ's staff to minimize audit costs.
  - Comment on the impact of transition on XYZ staff.
- Provide a list of other not-for-profit association clients most similar to XYZ. Explain their similarities and provide the name and telephone number of a contact person.
- State the date of your last peer review and the results.
- State your fees for the services described.

Required Services and Bid Amount

XYZ is requesting a 3-year bid from your firm to

- Conduct an audit and provide your opinion of XYZ's financial statement beginning with the year ended May 31, 20XX.
- Prepare a management letter, including client responses to the comments, for distribution to the board of directors. A representative of the firm will meet with members of the board, typically during the summer meeting.
- Hold an exit interview with the executive director and chief financial officer to review copies of the above reports before such reports are presented to governance representatives.
- Prepare Forms 990 and 990-T and related state income tax returns.
- Conduct an audit of the association's two benefit plans.

Appendix 6.B

Sample Client Assistance Request List

March 10, 20XX

Mr. CFO
XYZ Association
5678 Association Lane
Anytown, USA

Dear Mr. CFO:

Enclosed is a list of the items we are requesting from you and your staff in connection with our audits of your financial statements for the year ending May 31, 20XX. We expect to begin interim fieldwork on April 22, 20XX, and year-end fieldwork on June 27, 20XX. Please let me know as soon as possible if this timing does not meet your needs.

Please provide the items listed on the dates noted in the letter. Confirmations should be prepared, signed and returned to me for mailing with our business reply envelopes.

Feel free to contact me if you have any questions. Thank you in advance for your cooperation.

Sincerely,

Joe Auditor
CPA Firm

Enclosures

Audit Preparation Checklist—Interim Procedures
XYZ Association
May 31, 20XX

Please prepare the following supporting documents for fieldwork on April 22, 20XX:

1. Access to minutes of meetings of the board of directors and other related committees for the period from June 1, 20XW, to present.
2. Accounts-receivable detail at 03/31/XX. A sample will be selected for confirmations and subsequent receipt testing.
3. Trial balance for the 10 months ended March 31, 20XX.
4. Access to investment statements from throughout the year.
5. Detailed schedule of unbilled accounts receivable at 3/31/XX.
6. A listing of any additions or deletions to fixed assets from 6/1/XW to 03/31/XX as well as access to supporting invoices. If any were disposed of, please provide a schedule of gain or loss on the disposal.
7. A rollforward of notes payable showing all new borrowings and payments made, and access to supporting documentation.
8. Access to all legal invoices and a detail schedule of legal expenses paid during the year.
8. Copies of any new leases or other debt or significant contractual agreements.
10. Copies of any new pension plan documents or agreements.
11. Any new accounting or procedural manuals.
12. Summary schedule of meeting revenue and expenses for the annual convention. Please provide schedule of registration and exhibitor rates and number of attendees and exhibitors.
13. Summary of special program revenue and expenses by program. Please provide access to largest contracts and related promotional material.
14. We intend to perform a test of controls over disbursements. Please provide to us the sequence(s) of checks used from June 1, 20XW, to March 31, 20XX, so a sample can be selected prior to our arrival.
15. We also intend to perform a test of controls over payroll. Access to payroll records and personnel files will be requested on site.
16. We also intend to perform a test of cash receipts/revenue. Assistance will be required for pulling batches and tracing the recording of the revenue into the system.
17. Projection of inventory balances at 5/31/XX.

Audit Preparation Checklist—Year-End Procedures
XYZ Association
May 31, 20XX

The following items should be typed and returned to us for mailing *as soon as possible* (see enclosures):

1. Cash and broker confirmations for any bank or broker who maintained an account for XYZ at any time during the fiscal year ended May 31, 20XX (including certificates of deposit and deferred compensation accounts).
2. Legal confirmations for attorneys that have provided legal services to XYZ in FYXX.
3. Confirmation for the unsecured and secured lines of credit, and the notes payable.
4. Post-closing detail trial balance for the fiscal year ended May 31, 20XX, (on diskette).

Please prepare the following supporting documents for fieldwork on June 27, 20XX:

1. Bank reconciliations for all cash accounts, including supporting documentation (i.e. outstanding check lists, 05/XX & 06/XX bank statements (when available), and access to the FYXY check register).
2. A bank transfer schedule for all wire/check transfers greater than or equal to $10,000 from May 23, 20XX to June 7, 20XX if any.
3. Access to all bank statements from June 20XX to present.
4. Monthly investment analyses for FYXX. These schedules should include income and gains or losses (realized and unrealized) and supporting documentation (i.e. brokerage account statements). Please provide calculation of realized gains and losses on both a historical cost basis and revalued cost basis.
5. A schedule of accrued bond interest as of May 31, 20XX.
6. Roll-forward of investment in subsidiary account.
7. Accounts Receivable roll-forward schedule from March 31 to May 31. (This schedule should show the balances listed on the March 31 report we received previously, any additional receivables from 3/31 to 5/31, any cash receipts or write-offs during this time, and the balance as of 5/31. In addition, please provide documentation for any transaction over $61,000. Please reconcile to the trial balance, if necessary.
8. Accounts receivable detail schedule showing the number of days outstanding.
9. Deferred revenues by type; that is, membership dues, publication A, periodical B, prepaid conference fees, and so forth.
10. Please provide an average number of members during FYXX.
11. In the event that there has been an increase in membership dues, please provide authorizing documentation from the board of directors of the dues increase.
12. Analyses of special, royalty, and sponsorship income, including budget and prior-year comparisons. Please explain any major differences.
13. A detail schedule of accounts payable as of May 31, 20XX. The schedule should identify, by vendor, amounts due for services or goods received prior to May 31, 20XX. Please reconcile to the general ledger, if necessary.
14. Copies of June 20XX (through the end of fieldwork) cash disbursement registers.
15. A schedule of prepaid expenses.
16. General ledger detail for all accounts related to repairs or maintenance.
17. Budget and prior-years' comparative statement of activities. Please explain any major differences.
18. A detail schedule of accrued expenses as of May 31, 20XX, including accrued pension expense, accrued vacation, post retirement benefits, and other related expenses.
19. A schedule reconciling recorded salary expense to the federal Forms 941.

20. A schedule to support vacation liability as of 5/31/XX. Please also include the number of vacation hours accrued.
21. Support for the pension liabilities (401k match and defined-benefit plans).
22. Support for deferred-compensation balances.
23. A schedule detailing the quantity and price of inventory. Please reconcile to the trial balance, if necessary.
24. A listing of any additions or deletions to fixed assets from March 31 to May 31, and access to supporting invoices. In addition, we require a schedule of gain or loss on the disposal of any fixed assets, if applicable. Please also provide depreciation schedules for the year.
25. Summary of borrowings and repayments under line of credit.
26. A detailed schedule of notes payable. Please provide year-end loan invoice supporting balance due.
27. A detailed schedule of the income taxes payable, prepaid tax, and all income tax expense accounts. Please provide the UBIT supporting schedules provided in the past.
28. Rollforward of board-designated reserve accounts.
29. Copies of any new pension plan documents or agreements.
30. A detailed schedule of amounts supporting legal expense, rental expense (both office and equipment), and repairs and maintenance.
31. Copies of any new leases or other debt or significant contractual agreements.
32. Access to minutes of meetings of the board of directors and other related committees for the period from March 31, 20XX to present.
33. Any new accounting or procedural manuals.
34. Reconciliation of intercompany balances.

Tax Preparation Checklist
XYZ Association
May 31, 20XX

A. Schedule of contributions, gifts and grants received in excess of $5,000 during FYXX, including

   1. Contributor's name

   2. Contributor's address

   3. Date of contribution

   4. Contribution amount

B. Schedule of all assets sold, other than inventory, during FYXX, including

   1. Proceeds from the sale or disposal

   2. Original cost of the asset

   3. Accumulated depreciation up to the date of disposal

   4. Gain or loss on the sale or disposal

C. List of grants and allocations made to other organizations during the year, including name and amount and relationship, if any, to XYZ.

D. Update Parts III and VIII of Form 990—Statement of Program Service Accomplishments, and Relationship of Activities to the Accomplishment of Exempt Purposes.

E. Schedule of all compensated and noncompensated officers, directors, and trustees, including

   1. Title

   2. Average hours per week devoted to the position

   3. Compensation

   4. Contributions to employee benefit plans on their behalf

   5. Expense accounts and other allowances on their behalf

F. Answers to all questions listed on page 5 of the federal Form 990, including the amount of lobbying expenditures incurred by XYZ and the percentage of dues reported to members as nondeductible.

G. Operating expense analysis for XYZ converting expenses per the financial statements to the line items required on Form 990 Part II.

Appendix 6.C

Sample Representation Letter

July 15, 20XX

Mr. CFO
XYZ Association
5678 Association Lane
Anytown, USA

Dear Mr. CFO:

Enclosed is a "client representation letter" in which we have summarized information given to us verbally during the course of our engagement.

Please review this letter and, if you are in agreement with the facts as stated, return a signed copy to this office at your earliest convenience. After we receive this signed representation letter, we will issue your financial statements. If you wish to discuss any of the representations contained in this letter, please contact our office.

Sincerely,

CPA Firm
Certified Public Accountants

Enclosure

XYZ Association

July 15, 20XX

Mr. Partner, C.P.A.
CPA Firm
1234 Accounting Lane
Anytown, USA

Dear Mr. Partner:

We are providing this letter in connection with your audits of the financial statements of XYZ Association as of May 31, 20XX and 20XW, and for the years then ended, for the purpose of expressing an opinion as to whether the financial statements present fairly, in all material respects, the financial position, changes in net assets, and cash flows of XYZ Association in conformity with generally accepted accounting principles. We confirm that we are responsible for the fair presentation in the financial statements of financial position, changes in net assets, and cash flows in conformity with generally accepted accounting principles.

Certain representations in this letter are described as being limited to matters that are material. Items are considered material, regardless of size, if they involve an omission or misstatement of accounting information that, in the light of surrounding circumstances, makes it probable that the judgment of a reasonable person relying on the information would be changed or influenced by the omission or misstatement.

We confirm, to the best of our knowledge and believe, as of July 15, 20XX, the following representations made to you during your audits:

1. The financial statements referred to above are fairly presented in conformity with generally accepted accounting principles.
2. We have made available to you all of the following:
   a. Financial records and related data
   b. Minutes of meetings of directors, and committees of directors, or summaries of actions of recent meetings for which minutes have not yet been prepared
   c. Information relating to all statutes, laws, or regulations that have a direct effect on our financial statements
3. There have been no communications from regulatory agencies concerning noncompliance with or deficiencies in financial reporting practices.
4. There are no material transactions that have not been properly recorded in the accounting records underlying the financial statements.
5. Neither of the following has occurred:
   a. Fraud involving management or employees who have significant roles in internal control.
   b. Fraud involving others that could have a material effect on the financial statements.

6. The organization has no plans or intentions that may materially affect the carrying value or classification of assets and liabilities.

7. The following have been properly recorded or disclosed in the financial statements:

   a. Related-party transactions, including sales, purchases, loans, transfers, leasing arrangements, and guarantees, and amounts receivable from or payable to related parties.

   b. Guarantees, whether written or oral, under which the organization is contingently liable.

   c. Significant estimates and material concentrations known to management that are required to be disclosed in accordance with the AICPA's Statement of Position 94-6, *Disclosure of Certain Significant Risks and Uncertainties*. We understand that significant estimates are estimates at the balance-sheet date that could change materially within the next year. Concentrations refer to volumes of revenues, available sources of supply, or markets or geographic areas for which events could occur that would significantly disrupt normal finances within the next year.

8. None of the following activities have been observed:

   a. Violations or possible violations of laws or regulations whose effects should be considered for disclosure in the financial statements or as a basis for recording a loss contingency

   b. Unasserted claims or assessments that our lawyer has advised us are probable of assertion and must be disclosed in accordance with Financial Accounting Standards Board (FASB) Statement No. 5, *Accounting for Contingencies*

   c. Other liabilities or gain or loss contingencies that are required to be accrued or disclosed by FASB Statement No. 5

9. The organization has satisfactory title to all owned assets, and there are no liens or encumbrances on such assets nor has any asset been pledged as collateral, except as disclosed in the financial statements.

10. The organization has complied with all aspects of contractual agreements that would have a material effect on the financial statements in the event of noncompliance.

11. Provision, when material, has been made to

    a. Reduce excess or obsolete inventories to their estimated net realizable value.

    b. Reduce all investments for permanent declines in value.

    c. Adjust long-lived assets, certain identifiable intangibles, and related goodwill to their net fair value in accordance with FASB Statement No. 121 when the net cash flow from future uses of such assets indicate the recorded value is not expected to be recovered.

12. The organization is exempt from taxation under Section 501(c)(6) of the Internal Revenue Code and has not received any notices or other indications that the exempt status of the organization has been or will be challenged.

13. The bases for the allocation of functional expenses are, in our opinion, reasonable and consistent with the prior period.

14. The financial statements include all assets under our control and liabilities for which the organization has primary responsibility for settlement.

15. It is our belief that the effects of any uncorrected financial statement misstatements aggregated by you during the current engagement and pertaining to the latest period presented are immaterial, both individually and in the aggregate, to the financial statements taken as a whole. A summary of those audit differences is attached to and a part of this letter.

To the best of our knowledge and belief, no events have occurred subsequent to the balance-sheet date and through the date of this letter that would require adjustment to or disclosure in the aforementioned financial statements.

_____

(Chief Executive Officer)

_____

(Chief Financial Officer)

XYZ Association
Summary of Audit Differences
Year Ended May 31, 20XX

	Current-Year Over (Under) Statement
Statement of activities misstatements:	
Uncollectible accounts not reserved	$ 6,000
Compensated absences not accrued	4,000
Cumulative effect (before effect of prior-year differences)	10,000
Effect of unadjusted audit differences for prior year:	
Compensated absences not accrued	(3,000)
Cumulative effect (after effect of prior-year differences)	$ 7,000
Reclassification adjustments:	
Statement of financial position misstatements (including reclassifications):	
Current assets	$ 6,000
Total assets	6,000
Current liabilities	(4,000)
Total liabilities	(4,000)
Net assets:	
Beginning	3,000
Ending	10,000

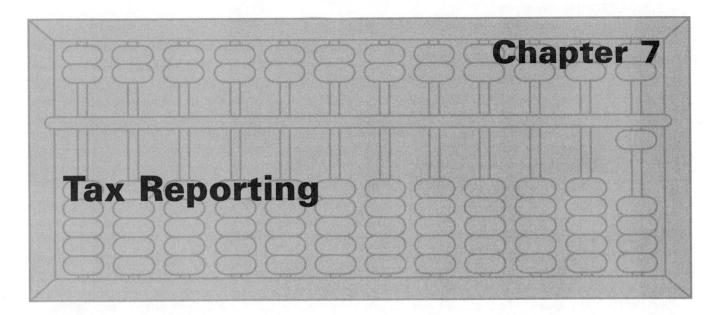

Chapter 7

Tax Reporting

Associations are typically exempt from taxes under either Section 501(c)(3) or 501(c)(6) of the Internal Revenue Code. In exchange for the benefit of not paying income taxes, the association or nonprofit must agree to abide by certain rules and file federal Form 990 on an annual basis.

This chapter will briefly cover the basics of obtaining tax-exempt status for Section 501(c)(3) and 501(c)(6) entities (which make up the lion's share of associations) and will review the requirements of filing federal Forms 990 and 990-T (for unrelated business income taxes). We will also cover briefly the rules for political action committees.

Obtaining Tax-Exempt Status

Nonprofit organizations are not automatically exempt from federal income taxes. Most organizations seeking recognition of tax exemption must complete the application forms required by the IRS, which are currently Form 1023 for Section 501(c)(3) entities and Form 1024 for 501(c)(6) organizations. Although it is not necessarily required for a Section 501(c)(6) entity to file Form 1024, it is generally recommended to ensure the peace of mind of an IRS determination letter. Except for certain church-related Section 501(c)(3) entities, it is necessary to file Form 1023 and receive a determination letter.

Ongoing Tax-Exempt Status

Maintaining tax-exempt status generally requires that an organization continue to function for the purposes for which it was established and that there is no private inurement of the benefits of the organization to any individual or select group (whether employees, members, or others) within the association. Some of the types of activities to watch out for would include the following:

- Unrelated business activities becoming too large a part of the association's budget—there is no set percentage to make this determination; it is strictly a facts and circumstances test.
- Not adhering to rules and regulations with respect to political activities.
- Excessive compensation or benefits or payments to employees or others in a position to control the amount they are paid or allocated.
- Failure to comply with antitrust rules and regulations—clandestine and secretive business practices that are anticompetitive or benefit a select group within the association.
- Engaging in criminal activities.

Section 501(c)(6) Entities

Section 501(c)(6) entities (business leagues, chambers of commerce, real estate boards, etc.) have been granted exemptions since the first federal income tax laws were written. To be considered exempt, these entities must not be organized for profit, and no part of the net earnings may inure to the benefit of any private shareholder or individual. It must be an association of persons having some common business interest, and its purpose must be directed to the improvement of businesses conditions of one or more lines of business as distinguished from the performance of particular services for individual persons or entities. It is permissible for Section 501(c)(6) organizations to engage in international activities, and there are no specific limitations on how much lobbying a Section 501(c)(6) organization can engage in. There is no provision for individuals or corporations to deduct "charitable contributions" to Section 501(c)(6) entities, although membership dues and other payments are generally deductible by corporations as ordinary and necessary business expenses.

Section 501(c)(3) Entities

In addition to being exempt from income tax on activities related to their exempt purpose, Section 501(c)(3) entities also enjoy certain other distinct benefits as follows:

- They are eligible to receive tax-deductible charitable contributions.
- They are more likely to be eligible to receive grants from private foundations, corporations, and federal, state, and local governments.
- They may be able to qualify for nonprofit postal permits.
- They are more likely to be eligible to receive various state tax exemptions such as sales and use tax, personal property tax, and real property tax.
- The are eligible to issue tax-exempt bonds.

On the other hand, there are some additional limitations on being a Section 501(c)(3) entity. Namely, there is a complete ban on Section 501(c)(3) organizations engaging in political activities, and there are limitations on the extent of lobbying activities that may be conducted.

A Section 501(c)(3) entity must be operated primarily for charitable, religious, educational, literary, scientific, or certain other purposes. One often thinks of Section 501(c)(3) organizations as being churches, charities, museums, or private schools. The IRS has ruled, however, that professional society membership organizations can be Section 501(c)(3)s provided that their purposes are to advance the profession by engaging in exclusively educational activities.

Section 501(c)(3)s must also meet certain other organizational and operational tests. One of the most important is the dissolution test, whereby if the organization dissolves, its assets must be distributed in furtherance of its exempt purposes or to the federal, state, or local government for a public purpose.

Section 501(c)(3) entities are also classified as either public charities or private foundations, depending on the diversification of funding they receive. It would generally be easy for membership organizations with a large base of members to qualify as a public charity. Operating as a private foundation would subject the entity to some additional operating complexities and certain taxes not applicable to public charities.

IRS Audits

Obviously, one of the business issues that exists for any business or association is the possibility of an IRS audit. Your organization could be selected on a truly random basis, as a result of some specific issues about your organization that the IRS wants to investigate, or because associations are part of the IRS work plan for a particular year. As with most audits, larger organizations in terms of asset base or annual revenue have a higher chance of being selected.

As might be expected, the best defense for an IRS audit is to have very accurate accounting records that fully support all the items on your filed Form 990 or 990-T return. The agent will generally be looking to see that the organization is operating in accordance with your purported tax-exempt status as outlined in your originally filed tax-exempt application and in your subsequent Form 990 filings. They will also be looking for any unreported unrelated business income items (e.g., if the association had advertising and didn't report it on the 990-T) and for supporting backup for revenues and expenses reported on the 990-T. They could also conceivably look at a host of payroll and profit-sharing plans as well as other items in your organization, depending on the type of audit being conducted.

We would generally advise that the association have a CPA experienced in IRS audits act as your agent in interacting with the IRS examiner and limit the agent's access to records the IRS has specifically requested. Of course, the easiest audit on your behalf will result if your records are in good shape and the auditor can easily conduct their examination.

Accounting Periods and Methods

Associations choose their annual accounting period with the filing of their first tax return. New organizations can choose as their annual accounting period a fiscal year ending on the last day of any month other than December or a calendar year-end. There are several factors to consider in selecting a fiscal year, such as whether a natural business year exists (e.g., coinciding your year-end around a major conference) or whether a calendar year would be best.

The election to adopt a year-end is made by the timely filing of the first tax return (Form 990) by the due date of the return (including timely filed extensions). If necessary, it is not too difficult to change year-ends. An association's method of accounting (cash, accrual) is also determined on the basis which the first tax return is filed.

Form 990

In general, all tax-exempt organizations (except churches) are required to file Form 990 unless their average annual gross receipts are less than $25,000. Most organizations will file Form 990; however, those with gross receipts of less than $250,000 may file Form 990-EZ. All nonprofit organizations described in Section 501(c)(3), other than private foundations, are also required to file Schedule A along with this Form 990.

Filing Dates

Form 990 or 990-EZ has an original due date of the fifteenth day of the fifth month of the organization's tax year (May 15 for a calendar-year entity). If the regular due date falls on a Saturday, Sunday, or legal holiday, the return should be filed on the next business day. The return should be filed with the IRS in Ogden, Utah.

Organizations can receive total extensions of the filing deadline of up to 6 months by filing Form 2758. Extension requests are only granted 3 months at a time, so a calendar-year organization should complete extensions at May 15 and August 15 to have until November 15 to complete the return.

It is extremely important to properly file all required extensions and timely file the Form 990 because severe penalties can result from failure to do so. Organizations with annual gross receipts exceeding $1 million can be subject to a penalty of $100 per day (with a maximum penalty with respect to any one return of $50,000). Although the IRS may waive penalties in some situations, it is not something you should try. Make sure the returns are filed on time.

Components of Form 990

Form 990 is used to report a wide variety of data, including basic financial information and the program service accomplishments of the organization. Although most associations have the Form 990 prepared by their CPA firm, it is helpful to be familiar with the elements of the return. The components of the Form 990 are as follows:

Part I—Revenue, Expenses, and Changes in Net Assets
  Part I outlines the information included in the association's statement of activities and provides considerable details related to the sources of an organization's revenue.
Part II—Program Services, Management, and General and Fund-Raising Expenses
  Part II presents a statement of functional expenses with expenses broken down into categories of program services, management, general, and fund-raising. The complete statement of functional expenses is only required for Section 501(c)(3) and 501(c)(4) entities and is optional for other entities, such as Section 501(c)(6)

entities. Generally Section 501(c)(6) entities provide only total expense information not broken down in the three categories. Program services expenses are the costs associated with the activities of the association related to their exempt purposes and can also include their unrelated business activities. Management and general expenses are those costs related to the overall management of the organization, as opposed to any specific program or fund-raising activity. The expenses include items such as the executive officer's time spent on general management matters, meetings of the board and committees on general matters, corporate legal services, general accounting and auditing, personnel administration, and centralized services. Fund-raising expenses relate to the expenses incurred in soliciting contributions. These costs include publicizing and conducting fund-raising campaigns, soliciting bequests and grants, and preparing and distributing fund-raising materials.

Part III—Statement of Program Service Accomplishments

Part III is where associations state what their primary exempt purpose is and state their program service accomplishments during the year. This is particularly important for Section 501(c)(3) entities that raise contributions from the general public. They want to describe all their accomplishments in as much detail and in as glowing terms as possible, especially because many Section 501(c)(3) returns are on the Internet at www.guidestar.org. To the extent that details regarding the exempt accomplishments are quantifiable, that information should be provided (i.e., number of clients served, publications produced, conferences held, and so forth). This disclosure is necessary for the IRS to determine that the entity is still operating consistently with the exempt purposes outlined in its original exemption application and for reporting any activity changes.

Part IV—This part requires organizations to provide comparative balance sheets on the last day of the current and prior fiscal year along with supporting schedules of various balance-sheet accounts.

Parts IV-A and IV-B—Reconciliation Statements

These parts of the Form 990 are used to reconcile differences between the organization's financial statements and the financial numbers used in Part I of Form 990. If the organization does not have an audited financial statement, they would mark this section "N/A."

Part V—List of Officers, Directors, Trustees, and Key Employees.

This part of Form 990 provides compensation information for the key individuals within the organization. Each person who was an officer, director, trustee, or other key employee at any time during the year should be listed. A key employee includes any personnel having responsibilities or powers similar to those of an officer, director, or trustee. Generally, this would include the executive director or chief management official and possibly the chief financial officer or the officer in charge of program operations, if those employees have the authority to control the organization's activities, finances, or both. This part also calls for compensation information to be listed for those positions. Compensation includes salaries, fees, bonuses, severance pay amounts received during the year, and compensation that was deferred in a prior year and paid during the current year. Contributions to employee benefit plans and fringe benefit payments are included as well.

Part VI—Other Information

In Part VI, organizations are required to answer questions related to various factors about their exempt status. New exempt activities the association is engaged in should be reported, and questions about whether the organization incurred any political expenditures, complied with IRS public inspection requirements, and so forth should be addressed. There are also a series of questions regarding the requirement that tax-exempt organizations other than those described in Section 501(c)(3) send notices to their members specifying the portion of their dues allocable to lobbying or to pay a "proxy tax" if this notification is not made. These requirements will be discussed in greater detail later in this chapter.

Part VII—Analysis of Income Producing Activities and Part VIII—Relationship of Activities to Accomplishment of Exempt Purposes

Parts VII and VIII of Form 990 analyze sources of the association's revenue other than contributions for the purposes of determining if the primary source of its revenue is from exempt purpose activities or from unrelated business income activities.

Part VII shows the apportionment of gross revenue other than contributions among the following categories: unrelated business income; revenue specifically excluded from unrelated business income in IRS Code

Sections 512, 513, or 514; and the income related to the exempt activities of the association. Revenue specifically excluded from unrelated business income taxes (UBIT) in Code Sections 512 through 514 is described in an exclusion code list included in the Form 990 instructions, shown in Appendix A. These codes display items that Congress has specifically decided will not be subject to UBIT. Related or exempt function income relates to income from the activities that form the basis of the organization's exemption from taxation. These types of items for an association would include membership dues, convention and conference revenue, publication sales, and so forth. These items are described to the IRS in Part VIII. Other remaining income would be that subject to UBIT.

Part IX—Information Regarding Taxable Subsidiaries

This question gathers some general information on associations that have a 50% or greater interest in a taxable corporation or partnership.

Schedule A of Form 990

For applicable organizations, Schedule A to Form 990 is required to be filed to satisfy the timely filed requirement. Organizations required to file Schedule A include Section 501(c)(3) entities (other than private foundations and certain other charitable type organizations). Section 501(c)(4) and 501(c)(6) organizations are not required to file Schedule A. The parts of the Schedule A are as follows:

Part I—Compensation of the Five Highest Paid Employees Other than Officers, Directors, and Trustees

This part requires the same type of information stated in Part V of Form 990 for employees who were not listed in Part V. Detailed information is presented for the five highest paid employees receiving over $50,000, and the total number of other employees receiving over $50,000 is also required.

Part II—Compensation of the Five Highest Paid Independent Contractors for Professional Services

This requires information about payments made to independent contractors (whether individuals or firms) who performed personal services and were paid over $50,000 for the year as well as the total number of other contractors paid over $50,000 who were not separately listed. Personal services would be services performed by attorneys, accountants, computer consultants, doctors, or fund-raising consultants, and other such professionals.

Part III—Statements about Activities

This part asks certain questions aimed primarily at determining whether the Section (c)(3) organization engages in an insubstantial amount of lobbying activities or whether it engaged in any inappropriate transactions with insiders to the organization. The lobbying requirements for Section 501(c)(3) organizations will be discussed later in this chapter. Other questions are aimed at determining whether there were transactions with insiders where "private inurement" may have occurred.

Part IV—Reason for Non–Private Foundation Status

This schedule determines whether an organization still qualifies for public charity status as opposed to private foundation status. This part of the schedule can be very complicated, and private foundation status is generally not an issue for associations, so it will not be discussed here at any great length.

Part V—Private School Questionnaire

Relates to questions aimed at determining that the school does not maintain a racially discriminatory policy towards their students.

Part VI—Lobbying Expenditures by Electing Public Charities or Lobbying Activity by Non-Electing Public Charities

Lobbying activities of Section 501(c)(3) entities is discussed in the "Lobbying by Section 501(c)(3) Entities" section later in this chapter.

Part VII—Information Regarding Transfers to and Transactions and Relationships with Non-Charitable Exempt Organizations

This part is aimed at determining if tax-deductible contributions to charities are being improperly transferred to non-charitable exempt organizations, such as Section 501(c)(4) or 501(c)(6) entities.

Lobbying

The 1993 Tax Act changed the landscape for associations with respect to lobbying activities. For federal tax purposes, taxpayers can no longer deduct any lobbying expenditures. In addition, associations are required to report to their members what portion of their dues is related to lobbying and would, therefore, be nondeductible or would require them to pay a proxy tax of 35% on lobbying expenditures. These rules apply to Section 501(c)(4), 501(c)(5), and 501(c)(6) organizations only; they do not apply to Section 501(c)(3) entities. There are also limited exceptions for associations incurring only de minimis in-house lobbying expenses of $2,000 or less or for organizations whose member dues are substantially nondeductible. The exception for organizations whose members would generally not be taking a business deduction for dues applies to the following types of organizations:

- All organizations exempt from tax under Section 501(a), other than Section 501(c)(4), (5), or (6) organizations. For example, a Section 501(c)(3) organization is exempt.
- Local associations of employees and veterans' organizations described in Section 501(c)(4) but not other social welfare organizations.
- Certain labor organizations.
- Section 501(c)(4), (5), and (6) organizations who receive more than 90% of their dues from Section 501(c)(3) organizations, state governments, and local governments.
- Section 501(c)(4), (5), and (6) organizations that receive more than 90% of their annual dues from persons, families, or entities who paid dues of $77 or less (adjusted for inflation).
- Organizations who do not have a membership.

If one of the exceptions is not available, associations must disclose to their members what estimated percentage of their dues would be nondeductible at the beginning of the year and then must report on the Form 990 the actual expenses incurred compared to this estimate.

An association that chooses not to report to its members could alternatively elect to pay a proxy tax on the total amount of its lobbying expenditures (up to the amount of dues and similar payments received by the organization during the year). Any excess of lobbying expenditures over dues and similar payments is carried forward to the next year. The proxy tax is payable at the highest corporate tax rate of 35% and is reported on the Form 990-T; otherwise, it is used as a tax return for unrelated business income.

If an organization's actual lobbying expenditures exceeded the amount reported in a timely notice of dues disallowance to members, it could either pay the proxy tax on the difference or agree to adjust its notice of lobbying expenses to members in the following year. If the association did not send the required dues notices in the reporting year, however, it must pay the proxy tax. The kinds of items that are considered lobbying are

- Influencing legislation—Any attempt to influence legislation through communications with any member of Congress, any member or employee of a state legislature, or any federal or state government official or employee who may participate in the formulation of legislation.
- Grassroots lobbying—Any attempt to influence the general public or segments thereof with respect to elections, legislative matters, or referenda.
- Communications to covered federal executive branch officials, including the president, vice-president, cabinet-level officials, and others.
- Political activities—Any activity that constitutes participation in or intervention in any political campaign on behalf of (or in opposition to) any candidate for federal office at the federal, state, or local level; this does not include a political action committee of the organization.
- Supporting activities—Any research, preparation, planning, and coordination for the purpose of making a lobbying communication.

There are some exceptions for activities considered to be lobbying, such as merely determining the procedural status of legislation and certain other exceptions.

Cost Allocation

After determining what activities constitute lobbying, costs must be assigned to them. IRS regulations provide that an association can use any reasonable method to allocate costs to lobbying activities. The regulations also provide three examples of methods that would be considered reasonable. An example of one of the three methods is the ratio method. Under this method an association would compute its lobbying costs as the following: third-party costs attributable to lobbying, plus internal costs attributable to lobbying calculated by the ratio of lobbying labor hours,[1] divided by total labor hours, and that result multiplied by the total cost of operations. Third-party costs are defined as amounts paid or incurred in whole or in part for lobbying activities conducted by third parties, such as outside lobbyists, plus amounts paid for travel and entertainment related in whole or part to lobbying activities. For example, if an organization spent $150,000 on third-party costs and 20% of their total labor hours were lobbying hours and their total operational costs (exclusive of third party costs) were $3,000,000, then their total lobbying costs would be (.2) 3,000,000 + 150,000 = $750,000.

Lobbying by Section 501(c)(3) Entities

The Internal Revenue Code for Section 501(c)(3) entities has provided for some time that "no substantial part of an organization's activities can constitute the carrying on of propaganda or otherwise attempting to influence legislation." The IRS regulations provide that the term *legislative* includes "action by the Congress, by any state legislature, by any local counsel or similar governing body, or constitutional amendment, or similar procedure." Attempts to influence legislation include direct lobbying, such as direct communication to members of the legislature, and also indirect or grassroots lobbying via communications through the general public. Prior to 1976, the determination of whether attempts to influence legislation comprised a "substantive portion" of an organization's total activities was based on a facts and circumstances test, which was subject to interpretation.

To clear up some of the confusion, Congress enacted Internal Revenue Code Sections 501(h) and 4911 as part of the Tax Reform Act of 1976. The purpose was to set relatively specific expenditure limits for lobbying activities to replace the unclear "no substantial part" test. The act also provided for a 25% excise tax on expenditures that exceeded the permissible level and for revocation of exempt status for an unreasonable excess over a period of time.

The provisions of Sections 501(h) and 4911 are only available to those eligible charities that make a voluntary election to be governed by those sections. Section 501(c)(3) entities could choose to not make this election and therefore would be subject to the "no substantial part" test. Most experts agree that Section 501(c)(3) entities are better off making the election unless they are very large organizations or engage in a disproportionate amount of grassroots lobbying. Eligible Section 501(c)(3) entities can make the election merely by filing Form 5768, "Election Revocation of Election by an Eligible Organization to Make Expenditures to Influence Legislation." The election is effective with the beginning of the taxable year in which the form is filed. Section 501(h) provides a sliding scale of permissible "lobbying nontaxable amounts" computed for both total and grassroots lobbying. Lobbying expenditures below these amounts are permissible and will result in neither an excise tax nor revocation of exempt status. Lobbying expenditures in excess of the permissible amounts are "excess lobbying expenditures" and are subject to an excise tax. Revocation of exempt status is possible if the amounts spent on lobbying "normally" exceed 150% of either the permissible total or grassroots lobbying amounts over a 4-year period.

The nontaxable amount of lobbying expenditures for electing organizations is the lesser of 1 million dollars or an amount determined in Table 7.1. The permissible amount of grassroots lobbying expenditures is 25% of the nontaxable amount of lobbying expenditures.

An excise tax is imposed on the excess lobbying expenditures of electing charities. The tax is equal to 25% of the amount of the organization's excess lobbying expenditures for the taxable year. This could occur by exceeding the total limit or by exceeding the grassroots limit. Organizations that normally make lobbying or grassroots

---

[1]The rules apply a de minimis for labor hours, whereby an organization can treat as zero situations where an individual spends less than 5% of their time lobbying.

Table 7.1 Nontaxable Amounts of Lobbying Expenditures

Exempt Purpose Expenditures	Total Nontaxable	Grassroots Nontaxable
Up to $500,000	20%	5%
$500,000–$1,000,000	$100,000 + 15% of excess over $1,000,000	$25,000 + 3.75% of excess over $500,000
$1,000,00–$1,500,000	$175,000 + 10% of excess over $1,000,000	$43,750 + 2.50% of excess over $1,000,000
$1,500,000–$17,000,000	$225,000 + 5% of excess over $1,500,000	$56,250 + 1.25% of excess over $1,500,000
Over $17,000,000	$1,000,000	$250,000

expenditures in excess of the *applicable ceiling amounts* risk losing their exempt status. The applicable ceiling amounts are 150% of the lobbying nontaxable amounts or 150% of the grassroots lobbying taxable amounts over a 4-year period.

Lobbying expenditures for electing public charities are defined as expenditures made for the purpose of influencing legislation. The total annual lobbying expenditures for an organization are the sum of its direct lobbying expenditures and grassroots expenditures. *Direct* lobbying includes attempts to influence legislation through communication with any member or employee of a legislative body. It also includes attempts to influence legislation through communication with any governmental official or an employee who may participate in the formation of the legislation, if the principal purpose of the communication is to influence legislation. *Grassroots* lobbying involves attempts to influence legislation by affecting the opinions of the general public or any segment of the general public.

There are a myriad of other regulations defining all these terms. One other advantage to making the election, however, is that for electing organizations certain activities are excluded from the term *influencing legislation,* such as dissemination of the results of nonpartisan analysis, study, or research; certain appearances before legislative bodies; provision of technical advice; or assistance in response to a written request by a governmental body and certain other activities.

Lobbying Disclosure Act of 1995

The Lobbying Disclosure Act of 1995 requires an organization to register and file semiannual reports detailing its lobbying activities if it has at least one employee who qualifies as a "lobbyist" as defined by the law and if the organization expects to spend $20,000 or more in a 6-month period in furtherance of lobbying activities. A *lobbyist* is defined as any person who, during either the January through June or the July through December period, (a) makes more than one lobbying contact with a "covered government official" and (b) engages in lobbying activities that consume at least 20% of such employee's time.

Group Exemptions

A group exemption letter is a ruling or determination letter issued by the IRS to a "central organization" recognizing on a group basis the federal tax exemption of affiliated "subordinate organizations" on whose behalf the central organization has applied for recognition of tax exemption. The group exemption is only applicable and necessary when the subordinate organizations are separate legal entities. This usually occurs to provide recognition of tax exemption on a group basis, for state and local chapters of national associations. It could also be used to provide group tax exemption for a state organization (even if it is a member of a national) and its affiliated local chapters.

Provided that the central organization has obtained its own tax-exempt status, it can apply for a group exemption letter for its affiliated subordinates under its supervision or control. The application is made by letter instead of by Form 1023 or 1024. The regulations provide all the information that must be included in the letter.

The procedures by which a group exemption may be recognized by the IRS require a functioning of the central organizations as an agent of the IRS. The central organization is required to continuously evaluate the tax-exempt status of its subordinate organizations to ensure that the tests for tax exemptions continue to be met by the subordinates. On an annual basis, the central organization is required to file a current listing of its qualifying subordinate organizations. This listing is effectively an attestation by the central organization that the subordinates continue to qualify as tax-exempt so that the IRS need not carry out an independent evaluation as to the tax-exempt status of the organization.

Annual Information

To maintain a group exemption, the central organization must submit the following information to the IRS on an annual basis, at least 90 days before the close of its annual accounting period:

- All changes (if any) in the purposes, character, or method of operation of the subordinates included in the group exemption.
- A separate list of the names, addresses, and employer identification numbers (EINs) of the affected subordinates for each of the following three categories:
  - Subordinates that have changed their names or address during the year.
  - Subordinates that should no longer be included in the group exemption because they no longer exist or have disaffiliated or withdrawn their authorization to the central organization, and subordinates to be added to the group exemption because they are newly organized or affiliated or because they have authorized the central organization to include them during the year.
  - If there were none of the above changes, the central organization must submit a statement to that effect.
  - For new subordinates to be added to the group, the information is required to be submitted by a central organization at the outset on behalf of subordinates.

Group exemption does not require that the subordinates file their Form 990 in combination with the central organization. Most national organizations require their chapters to file their own Form 990 returns each year if they are required. However, if desired, a group return on Form 990 may be filed by a central organization for two or more subordinates, and not all subordinates need be included. In this event, all financial data for the subordinates is included in the group return. This group return is filed in addition to the central organization's separate annual return, if required.

Intermediate Sanctions

In 1996, the intermediate sanctions law was signed into law. The direct applicability of the law is limited to Section 501(c)(3) and 501(c)(4) organizations, although the prohibition of "private inurement" also applies to Section 501(c)(5) and 501(c)(6) entities. Under the law, excise taxes can be imposed on excess benefit transactions. These are any transactions in which a Section 501(c)(3) or 501(c)(4) organization provides an economic benefit to a disqualified person that has a greater value than what it receives from the person. This would include providing compensation to a person in excess of the value of the services rendered or buying or renting property from a person for more than the property's fair market sale or rental value. The excess benefit equals the difference of the value of the benefit provided to the person over the value of the consideration received by the organization.

Excise taxes can be imposed in two different ways. The first is imposed on disqualified persons who receive an excess benefit. The tax is equal to 25% of the excess benefit. There is an additional tax equal to 200% of the benefit if it is not corrected before the date an IRS deficiency notice is mailed for the 25% tax or the date the 25% tax is assessed, whichever comes first. The second tax is imposed on organization managers who knowingly, willfully, and without reasonable cause participate in the excess benefit transaction. The tax is equal to 10% of the excess benefit but no more than $10,000. A disqualified person is someone who was in a position to exercise substantial influence over the affairs of the organization, which could include related parties to the disqualified person.

Compensation for services rendered will not be an excess benefit if it is an amount that would ordinarily be paid for similar services in a comparable situation. There is a presumption of reasonableness with respect to compensation or property sale or rental that Section 501(c)(3) or 501(c)(4) organizations should take advantage of, provided they meet the following requirements:

- The compensation or property sale or rental must be approved by the organization's governing body or by a committee of the governing body composed entirely of individuals who do not have a conflict of interest with respect to the transaction.
- The governing body or its committee must have obtained and relied upon appropriate data as to comparability prior to making its decision.
- The governing body or its committee must have adequately documented the basis for its decision at the time it was made.

The rules governing intermediate sections are complex, and organizations should coordinate with counsel to make sure they are protected in this area.

Unrelated Business Income Taxes (UBIT)

Although associations and other Section 501(c) entities are generally exempt from income taxes on the performance of activities related to their exempt purposes, they are potentially taxable on income derived from unrelated business activities. The UBIT is generally imposed on the federal corporate income tax rates (see Table 7.2). Deductions are permitted for expenses that are directly connected with the carrying on of the unrelated trade or business. If an organization regularly carries on two or more unrelated business income activities, its unrelated business taxable income (UBTI) is the total of the gross income from all such activities less the total allowable deductions attributable to such activities. The income will be considered unrelated business income if it meets the following three requirements:

1. It is considered income from a trade or business.
2. The business activity is regularly carried on.
3. The income is not substantially related to the purposes for which the organization was granted tax exemption.

Trade or Business Requirement

A trade or business is generally an activity carried on for the production of income from the sale of goods or the performance of services. The income generated must be active income; income from a passive activity is not considered a business.

Another basic principle of UBIT is the fragmentation rule, which stipulates that an activity does not lose its identity as a trade or business merely because it is carried on within a larger complex of other endeavors that may or may not be related to the exempt purposes of the organization. The typical association example for application of the fragmentation rule is advertising in a monthly association periodical. The advertising activity would be regarded as a trade or business even though the newsletter's subject matter relates to the association's tax-exempt purposes.

Activities Regularly Carried On

The regulations state that the frequency and continuity of the activities must be examined to make the determination of whether the activity is regularly carried on. Specific business activities will ordinarily be deemed to be reg-

Table 7.2   Federal Corporate Income Tax Rates

Annual Taxable Income	Tax Rate
$0–$50,000	15%
$50,001–$75,000	25%
$75,001–$100,00	34%
$100,001–$335,000	39%
$335,001–$10,000,000	34%
$10,000,001–$15,000,000	35%
$15,000,001–$18,333,333	38%
$18,333,334 and over	35%

ularly carried on if they manifest a frequency and continuity and are pursued in a manner generally similar to comparable commercial activities of nonexempt organizations. Activities carried only once per year, such as advertising in the program of an annual dinner dance may not be considered to be regularly carried on. On the other hand, an activity occurring only once a year might be considered to be regularly carried on if a commercial company performing the same activity would also only be active once a year.

Income Not Substantially Related to Exempt Purpose

Of the three UBIT factors this one is probably the most contested. This test requires that an organization review the relationship between the business activities that generated the income and the accomplishment of the organization's tax-exempt purpose. The substantial relationship to the organization's tax-exempt propose cannot come solely from the organization's need for money. How the money is used by the organization is also irrelevant as to whether a substantial relationship exists.

With respect to trade or professional organizations, an activity will be substantially related if it is directed toward the improvement of its members business conditions as opposed to the performance of particular services that provide a benefit to individual members in their businesses.

Some key factors also considered by the IRS in the context include

- The associations intent in performing the activity
- Whether the activity is comparable to activities conducted by commercial entities
- The uniqueness or distinctiveness of the activity to the association's tax-exempt purposes

In some cases, it may be possible to restructure the activities so that they would be related to an organization's exempt purpose.

Directly Connected Deductions

Deductions are allowed against the unrelated business income to arrive at the net income subject to tax. Expenses, depreciation, and other similar items attributable solely to the conduct of unrelated business activities are allowable to the extent that they are proximately and primarily related to that business activity and would otherwise be allowable as a deduction under the Internal Revenue Code. Expenses must also be determined under the tax principles applied to regular taxable corporations, such as depreciation charges.

Where facilities and personnel are used for both unrelated business activities and for exempt purposes, the expenses, depreciation, and the other items should be allocated between the two uses on a reasonable basis. There are also some special rules related to expenses from the exploitation of an exempt activity. These will be reviewed in the context of advertising income later in the chapter.

Modifications and Exclusions

Even if all three conditions of the UBIT test are satisfied, there are certain modifications and exclusions that could prevent activities from being UBTI. Some of those exceptions are the following:

- Dividends, interest, and annuities—Passive income received in the form of dividends, interest, and annuities along with any deductions related thereto would generally be excluded in computing UBTI. Exceptions to this exclusion can apply in cases where the investment income comes from debt-financed property or certain transactions with controlled organizations. For example, if an organization borrowed money to purchase investments, the income from the investments would be debt-financed and could be partially taxable.
- Activities performed with volunteer labor—UBTI does not include trade or business income in which substantially all the work in carrying on such trade or business is performed for the organization without compensation. *Substantially all* has generally been defined as 85% or more.
- Qualified convention or trade-show income—This exception relates to activities conducted by organizations described in Sections 501(c)(3), 501(c)(4), 501(c)(5), and 501(c)(6) that regularly conduct shows that stimulate interest in and demand for the products of a particular industry or segment of an industry or that edu-

cate the attendants regarding new developments or products and services related to the exempt activities of the organization. This would be the typical convention or conference of an association that has exhibitors, conferences, and seminars. The income received from the rental of the exhibit space, admissions to the show, and incidental income would be specifically excluded from UBTI. The advertising in a trade show directory might be considered UBTI, however.

Qualified Sponsorship Payments

The 1997 Tax Act stipulated that the receipt of "qualified sponsorship payments" by a tax-exempt organization does not constitute the receipt of income from an unrelated trade or business. A *qualified sponsorship payment* is defined as any payment of money, transfer of property, or performance of services by any person or entity engaged in a trade or business with respect to which there is no arrangement or expectation that the person will receive any substantial return benefit. Although the tax regulations discuss this in great detail, in general the typical substantial return benefit is advertising. As long as the corporate sponsor gets merely an acknowledgement and not the right to advertise, the sponsorship payment will not be subject to UBIT.

Advertising is defined as any message or other programming material that is broadcast or otherwise transmitted, published, displayed, or distributed and that promotes or markets any trade or business or any service, facility, or product. Advertising includes

- Messages containing qualitative or comparative language
- Price information or other indications of savings or value
- An endorsement
- An inducement to purchase, sell, or use any company, service, facility, or product

A single message that includes both advertising and an acknowledgement will be considered advertising.

Royalties

Royalties and the deductions directly connected with them are excluded in computing UBTI. This exclusion does not apply to debt-financed income or to royalties received from a controlled subsidiary. The IRS defines a royalty as any payment received in consideration of the use of a valuable intangible property right, whether or not that payment is based on the use made of the intangible property. Payment for the use of trademarks, trade names, service marks, copyrights, photographs, facsimile signatures, and members' names are ordinarily considered royalties.

Associations have battled in the courts as to the taxable or nontaxable nature of different endorsement and licensing arrangements, such as insurance program sponsorships, affinity credit cards, and membership list rentals. The court decisions tend to revolve around the activities of the association earning the income. If the association is actively involved in the program that gives rise to the income, then the IRS will consider the payment to be taxable income and not a royalty. If the role of the association is characterized as passive, the income will generally be excluded as a royalty. Associations entering into affinity endorsement programs should have counsel review the contracts and responsibilities to see whether the arrangement can be structured so that the association receives at least some (or all) tax-free royalty treatment for the payments instead of taxable payments for services.

Rental Income

Rents from real property are excluded in computing UBTI provided that the property is not debt-financed. Rents from personal property do not carry this exception and would be subject to UBIT.

Affiliations with Other Entities

There are many reasons why nonprofit organizations form affiliations with other entities. As nonprofit organizations are organized and approved to conduct a particular mission, they occasionally engage in an activity that could be perceived by the IRS as inconsistent with this mission. Other times an activity is perceived as being risky from the litigation standpoint, or an activity may generate so much unrelated business income that it could potentially harm their tax-exempt status. Occasionally, two nonprofits with a common interest want to carry on an activity, but neither one is appropriate to house the activity. For these and many other reasons, and in many other circumstances, nonprofits frequently find that to achieve a certain part of their purpose, the best way to accomplish their goal is through an affiliation with another entity.

There are many ways in which a nonprofit organization can affiliate itself with other entities to achieve certain purposes. The most common ones are summarized in the sections that follow.

Taxable Subsidiary

Nonprofit organizations have to carve out their income from activities that are considered unrelated to their mission, known as *unrelated business income,* and pay taxes on any net income that activity (or activities) produces. But what happens if the unrelated revenue of a particular nonprofit organization makes up a large percentage of its total revenues? Or what if an unrelated activity takes up a majority of staff time to administer? The tax-exempt status of the organization could be in jeopardy, because the organization is no longer considered to be primarily pursuing its tax-exempt purpose; it could be deemed to have become a competitive business instead. The IRS has the power to revoke tax-exempt status in such situations. Although neither the tax code nor the courts have committed to disclosing an actual percentage that tips the balance to defining a *substantial* activity, a preventative course of action is called for if a nonprofit organization perceives that it has an activity in question. To avoid such a catastrophe, many nonprofits will create a taxable subsidiary and place the unrelated business activity with the new entity. The for-profit company would pay taxes on its net income, and excess profits would be distributed to the parent nonprofit organization as tax-free dividends. The nonprofit organization can keep control of the taxable activity while protecting its tax-exempt status with the IRS.

Another good reason to spin off the unrelated business activity into a for-profit company is if the nonprofit organization fears that the product or service is susceptible to possible litigation and wants to protect the parent organization from possible litigation.

Establishing a taxable subsidiary is a serious undertaking that requires time, effort, and investment on behalf of the parent organization. The subsidiary must exist as independently as possible to remain viable. Initially, legal expenses of creating and incorporating the entity must be incurred, a separate board of directors assembled, separate accounting and cash accounts maintained, and a separate tax return filed annually in addition to all other applicable federal and state tax filings. The subsidiary must function under a substantial business reason and remain independent to be considered a viable business; otherwise, if it appears the nonprofit parent has virtually complete control, the IRS would have grounds to conclude that the subsidiary only exists for the parent organization's needs and potentially deem the subsidiary to not exist for tax purposes.

Joint Ventures and Partnerships

To stay competitive in the business arena today, many nonprofits, in particular member organizations and nonprofits in the health care field, have discovered that partnerships or joint ventures are a good way to provide for their members' changing needs; they also can provide an opportunity in the search for alternative sources of revenue. Often an opportunity not otherwise available to a nonprofit organization because of a limitation of resources can be obtained through a partnership or joint venture with a for-profit entity.

A joint venture is typically set up between a nonprofit and a taxable entity to conduct one transaction or one event. It does not typify an ongoing relationship; rather it has a finite purpose and timing. A partnership, on the other hand, is characterized by an ongoing, more permanent relationship.

A joint venture is taxed the same way as a partnership, which is to say they are not taxable, but all the income, gains, and losses retain their character and are treated as received by the owners. Therefore, in a joint venture or partnership, the nonprofit organization would be responsible for reporting income, gains, and losses on its tax return and in its financial statements. The nonprofit organization must consider the influence the activity may have on its tax-exempt status as well.

The activity engaged in by the joint venture or partnership must be evaluated to determine whether it is related to the nonprofit's mission or it is an unrelated business subject to the UBIT filing requirements, as though it was any of the nonprofit's other activities. All attributes of the activity need to be evaluated also to consider whether there is any affect on the tax-exempt status of the organization. Partnership income is often considered to be UBTI, however.

Political Action Committees

The tax laws and the federal election laws have made it either impossible or very expensive for nonprofit organizations to support political candidates or engage in making political expenditures. A Section 501(c)(3) nonprofit organization is prohibited from any direct political participation, whereas a 501(c)(6) is not prohibited but must pay a tax at the highest corporate rate on any political expenses incurred.

If a nonprofit organization wishes to conduct political fund-raising and incur political expenditures, it should establish a political action committee (PAC). A PAC is another specific type of nonprofit organization under the tax law. A PAC can solicit contributions from the nonprofit's members for support. The PAC can also legally make political contributions, and is not taxed on political income or expenditures. PACs are taxable on their non-political activity income and expenses, such as interest earned.

The earlier discussion regarding the time, effort, and investment required to establish a taxable subsidiary also applies to establishing a PAC. The PAC is a separate company and requires a certain level of administrative and financial attention to be run properly.

Chapters

Many national associations are represented in regional and local areas by smaller organizations with the same or similar mission, sometimes using the same name, and sometimes with overlapping or joint activities. The relationship between a national organization and its chapters can take a myriad of different forms.

The two most typical forms of organization are those in which the national is completely separate from the chapters or in which all entities are incorporated as one. When the national and chapter organizations are the same incorporated entity, the different locations are merely different office locations. The financial statements and tax return would report all the offices' income and expenses as one entity. In the other typical scenario, the national office merely encourages the establishment of chapters, who set up and incorporate separately. As separate entities, they should be incorporated individually, have their own boards of directors, management, and so forth.

The tax, legal, and operating ramifications vary as much as the organization style. One large organization with national and local offices needs to have financial and administrative control over the entire organization. The financial statements and tax return would be combined for all activities from all locations. If a national organization is incorporated separately from the chapters, the financial and administrative responsibilities of the national organization would be for itself. However, some responsibility to the chapters would still exist—there is much crossover between the two, but in a more nebulous manner. If name, mission, or activities are shared in any way, certainly some legal liability would also be construed as resting with the national organization for its chapter(s), which should not be ignored. Administrative control through policies and procedures should extend from this type of relationship.

The tax filing implications of a separate national organization from its chapters leaves some options available. A national organization can file its own federal Form 990, thus the chapters would be responsible for their own Form 990 tax filing. Or, the national organization can apply for a group affiliation number with the IRS and file a federal Form 990 for the group.

Association-Created Section 501(c)(3) Foundation

A business league, or Section 501(c)(6) under the tax code, is usually supported largely by member dues, which are deductible by its members as a business expense. A business league cannot receive tax-deductible contributions in accordance with the tax code. Frequently, a business league comes to a point in its operating life where it wants to solicit tax-deductible contributions, whether to fund a scholarship program or to somehow advance education or knowledge in the industry.

The solution for a business league in this situation is to establish a foundation in the form of a charitable organization, or Section 501(c)(3). As a subsidiary to the parent Section 501(c)(6) organization, or as a more loosely affiliated entity, the foundation can solicit contributions and make grants or scholarships to intended recipients and thus legally conduct the program or fulfill the need the business league wanted to promote without running afoul of the tax code.

The foundation must be set up and maintained as a viable and independent entity, whether it is deemed a subsidiary or becomes independent. An area that must be given good consideration is when the foundation makes grants to the Section 501(c)(6) organization. The foundation is not supposed to be controlled by the parent organization, thus the foundation's board of directors must have enough autonomy to determine recipients and in what amounts grants or scholarships will be made. If it appears to the IRS that the parent is exerting undue influence to collect grants, the foundation will be seen as merely a funnel for contributions and the foundation would risk losing its exempt status.

Unrelated Business Income

Nonprofit organizations apply for and are granted tax-exempt status if they qualify by showing a laundry list of documents and qualifications that are required, not the least of which is to have a mission. The programs and activities of the nonprofit organization go into supporting that tax-exempt mission. If the nonprofit organization has an activity that does not support it's mission, it is called an unrelated activity (i.e., unrelated to its mission) and the net income from that activity is taxable to the nonprofit organization. The tax return filed by Section 501(c)(3) and 501(c)(6) nonprofit organizations annually is the federal Form 990, "Return of Organization Exempt from Income Tax," which is an informational return, and does not include a tax calculation. If the nonprofit has engaged in an unrelated activity, the entity must also file a federal Form 990-T, "Exempt Organization Business Income Tax Return."

Following are brief descriptions of the most common types of unrelated business income.

Advertising Income

By far the most common type of unrelated business income generated by nonprofit organizations is advertising income. It is typical in the business of a nonprofit to produce a magazine, newsletter, or other type of periodical for it's members or to produce a brochure at a convention or meeting, and frequently advertising spaces are sold in these publications. The sale of advertising is considered an unrelated business by statute. Recent technology has seen the introduction of the Internet, as well as periodicals, as a medium for nonprofits to communicate with their members or the public, so advertising can also be sold for Web site space.

There are four terms for amounts whose definitions drive the calculation in order to determine net advertising income or loss, which is reported on the 990T. They are gross advertising income, direct advertising expense, readership costs, and circulation income.

Gross advertising income represents all income collected as a result of the advertising in a periodical or on the Internet. The direct advertising expenses are allowed to be subtracted against the advertising income to arrive at taxable net income. Direct expenses are those associated with the sale and production of the advertisement, such as salaries, printing, typesetting, production, and mailing.

If the advertising activity generates a net income after deducting the direct advertising costs from the gross advertising income, the nonprofit is then allowed to also deduct excess readership costs. Readership costs are the total cost of producing the periodical less the direct advertising costs already deducted. Excess readership costs are those that exceed the circulation income. Circulation income is generally the income collected from providing the periodical (or Web site) to the members or other users. For instance, if a subscription fee is charged for a magazine, the subscription income would be the circulation income. For a dues-charging member association that does not collect subscription fees, determining circulation income would entail prorating a portion of dues income to the periodical. If the circulation income is greater than readership costs, there is no additional deduction. If readership costs are greater than circulation income, the amount of the loss can be deducted from the net advertising income to the extent of net advertising income. A loss is not permitted from deducting excess readership costs. If the net advertising income is positive, losses from other unrelated business activities can be netted against it.

Example 7.1

X, an exempt trade association, publishes a single periodical that carries advertising. During 2002, X realizes a total of $40,000 from the sale of advertising in the periodical (gross advertising income) and $60,000 from sales of the periodical to members and nonmembers (circulation income). The total periodical costs are $90,000, of which $50,000 is directly connected with the sale and publication of advertising (direct advertising costs) and $40,000 is attributable to the production and distribution of the readership content (readership costs). Because the direct advertising costs of the periodical ($50,000) exceed gross advertising income ($40,000), the UBTI attributable to advertising is determined solely on the basis of the income and deductions directly connected with the production and sale of the advertising:

Gross advertising revenue	$40,000
Direct advertising costs	(50,000)
Loss attributable to advertising	($10,000)

X has realized a loss of $10,000 from its advertising activity. This loss is an allowable deduction in computing X's UBTI derived from any other unrelated trade or business activity.

Example 7.2

Assume the facts as stated in Example 7.1, except that the circulation income of X periodical is $100,000 instead of $60,000 and that of the total periodical costs $25,000 are direct advertising costs and $65,000 are readership costs. Because the circulation income ($100,000) exceeds the total readership costs ($65,000), the UBTI attributable to the advertising activity is $15,000, the excess of gross advertising income ($40,000) over direct advertising costs ($25,000).

Example 7.3

Assume the facts as stated in Example 7.1, except that of the total periodical costs $20,000 are direct advertising costs and $70,000 are readership costs. Because the readership costs of the periodical ($70,000) exceed the circulation income ($60,000), the UBTI attributable to advertising is the excess of the total income attributable to the periodical over the total periodical cost. Thus, X has UBTI attributable to the advertising activity of $10,000 ($100,000 total income attributable to the periodical less $90,000 total periodical costs).

Example 7.4

Assume the facts as stated in Example 7.1, except that the total periodical costs are $120,000, of which $30,000 are direct advertising costs and $90,000 are readership costs. Because the readership costs of the periodical ($90,000) exceed the circulation income ($60,000), the UBTI attributable to advertising is the excess, if any, of the total income attributable to the periodical over the total periodical costs. Because the total income of the periodical ($100,000) does not exceed the total periodical costs ($120,000), X has not derived any UBTI from the advertising activity. Further, only $70,000 of the $90,000 of readership costs may be deducted in computing UBTI, because such costs may be deducted to the extent they exceed circulation income only to the extent they do not result in a loss from the advertising activity. Thus, there is no loss from such activity, and no amount may be deducted on this account in computing X's unrelated trade or business income derived from any other unrelated trade or business activity.

Debt-Financed Income

Many nonprofit organizations own real estate for investment purposes, for use as office space by employees, or for program usage, such as a retreat property for religious organizations. Sometimes, in the course of business, nonprofit organizations rent out all or a portion of the properties they own.

If the property is owned free and clear, it is simply an investment generating investment income or for general use by the nonprofit, and there are no tax implications. But if there is a mortgage attached to the property, then the activity is deemed to be an unrelated business activity. The income generated from the property is known as debt-financed income.

A proportionate share of the rental income is taxable in proportion to the percentage of the value of the property that is mortgaged. Expenses are deducted in the proportionate amount also, such as depreciation, interest, real estate taxes, and office management expenses directly related to the property. The average acquisition indebtedness is divided by the average adjusted basis of the property during the year to calculate the percentage of income and expenses to report. If debt-financed real estate is sold, a portion of the gain will be subject to UBIT as well.

Example 7.5

X, an exempt trade association, owns an office building that produced $10,000 of gross rental income in 2002. The average adjusted basis of the building for 2002 is $100,000, and the average acquisition indebtedness with respect to the building for 2002 is $50,000. Accordingly, the debt/basis percentage for 2002 is 50% (the ratio of $50,000 to $100,000). Therefore, the unrelated debt-financed income with respect to the building for 2002 is $5,000 (50% of $10,000).

Loans to Controlled Organizations

If a nonprofit parent extends a loan to a controlled organization, the interest income received is considered unrelated business income by statute. For example, if a nonprofit parent organization loaned money to a for-profit subsidiary, the interest earned on the loan would be considered UBTI to the parent organization. Keep in mind that the for-profit sub will take a tax deduction for the interest paid, and without this provision (and others regulating payments between controlled organizations) would have an unfair tax advantage.

Group Insurance

Another common activity of member associations, and occasionally other types of nonprofit organizations, is to provide insurance programs to their members or a certain set of individuals. Often insurance costs can be kept to a minimum in these programs, thereby offering low premiums to the recipients. The insurance program can be set up in any way the organization chooses, from directly administering the insurance program to hiring an insurance company to handle all the tasks related to the program and merely pass along a percentage of the income to the nonprofit. The unrelated business income implications, however, vary widely depending on how it is set up. If the nonprofit is involved in the program, the IRS has taken the position that it is clearly an unrelated activity and is subject to UBIT. Although the guidelines are not completely clear within the tax law, it is fairly clear that if the nonprofit relinquishes management and administrative duties to an insurance administrator, the activity will not be considered unrelated. It would seem to be construed as similar to investment income if virtually all control were not maintained.

Form 990T

The federal Form 990T is due on the fifteenth day of the fifth month following the period end, the same filing deadline as the federal Form 990. Previously, there was an automatic 6-month extension available by filing a Form 8868 and checking the "990T" box, although at the time of this writing those rules are in flux and may require two separate 3-month extension requests—please consult your tax advisor for the latest information. The payment of tax is not extendable, however, and estimated amounts due must be paid with the extension. A separate Form 8868 should be filed for the 990T from the 990. Do not check more than one box for "type of return to be filed." Estimated tax payments may also be required throughout the year.

Example 7.6

The Association of Accountants for Accounting (the AAA) (not a real organization) is a Section 501(c)(3) membership organization. The mission of the association as approved by the IRS is to support, educate, and disseminate information to accountants. AAA has the following activities. The association publishes a bimonthly newsletter that includes sections of paid advertising. They hold an annual conference that includes educational seminars and an exhibit floor. They own an eight-story building where their management operations are located and rent out several of the floors to an unrelated third party. The association holds a mortgage for the building. A large investment portfolio has been accumulated over several years, which generates a healthy amount of income per year. Contributions are solicited for the scholarship fund, which is the reason the association formed as a Section 501(c)(3) and not a 501(c)(6).

AAA operates on a calendar-year basis, so their federal Form 990 is due on May 15 of every year. Two extensions are available for 3 months each, so it can be extended to August 15 and November 15 at the latest. AAA also files a federal Form 990-T, which is also due on May 15, with extensions available to November 15.

The association has determined that the advertising income it makes from the newsletter is unrelated business income, so management keeps an accounting of the income and related expenses so that they can report the net income from this activity on Form 990-T. A portion of membership dues is attributable to the newsletter, although management has to calculate an estimate for this amount because the newsletter is not sold separately. In years when the advertising income is more than the advertising expenses, the excess readership costs are then also calculated to report on Form 990-T as another subtraction (assuming the readership costs are greater than the circulation income).

The rental income received from the third party leasing space in the AAA's building is considered debt-financed income because a mortgage is held on the building. Therefore, the net income from this activity is considered an unrelated activity and must also be reported on Form 990-T. The expenses associated with the building, such as depreciation, interest, utilities, and staff time for management, are prorated for the square feet of the rented space to the total building square feet. Then the rental income and related expenses are prorated on the basis of the average mortgage balance to the average adjusted basis of the building during the year.

The income from member dues and conferences are considered tax-exempt because the services provided to the members through these activities directly supports the association's mission. The investment income from the portfolio is not considered UBTI because the tax code specifically exempts it.

Other Issues
Public Disclosure Requirements and Requests for Copies
A nonprofit's original application with the IRS (Forms 1023 or 1024) and the federal Form 990 for the last 3 years are open to public disclosure and inspection; certain rules as to exactly how to disclose apply.

If requested in person, generally the forms must be provided in person for review upon demand. If copies are requested, either in person or in writing, copies must be provided. A reasonable charge is allowed for the copying. If copies are requested in person, they must be provided right away. If the request comes in writing, the organization must comply within 30 days. The nonprofit has 7 days to request payment for the copy charge in advance, and then would have 30 days from the time of payment to provide the requested copies. An organization that posts its application for tax exemption and annual return information on a World Wide Web page may not have to comply with requests for copies of those documents.

Solicitation of Nondeductible Contributions
If a non–Section 501(c)(6) organization solicits contributions, the donor is not allowed under the tax law to take a charitable contribution deduction. Only Section 501(c)(3) organizations, which are charitable organizations, can be contributed to for the charitable tax deduction. For all other Section 501(c) organizations, there is a disclosure requirement that must be adhered to when soliciting contributions, because they are not deductible as charitable contributions. They may be business deductions for certain donors, but the particular taxpayer is at their own risk to make that determination. The IRS lists specific guidelines for how the disclosure of nondeductible contributions must be made. Generally speaking, the IRS dictates that it must be "conspicuous and easily recognizable." The IRS guidelines should be followed exactly when designing contribution solicitation material for a non–Section 501(c)(3) in order to avoid penalty.

Appendix 7.A

IRS Exclusion Codes for 990
Part VII

EXCLUSION CODES

General Exceptions

01 Income from an activity that is not regularly carried on (section 512(a)(1)).

02 Income from an activity in which labor is a material income-producing factor and substantially all (at least 85%) of the work is performed with unpaid labor (section 513(a)(1)).

03 Section 501 (c)(3) organization – Income from an activity carried on primarily for the convenience of the organization's members, students, patients, visitors, officers, or employees (hospital parking lot or museum cafeteria, for example) (section 513(a)(2)).

04 Section 501(c)(4) local association of employees organized before 5/27/69 - Income from the sale of work-related Clothes or equipment and items normally sold through vending machines; food dispensing facilities; or snack bar for the convenience of association members at their usual places of employment (section 513(a)(2)).

05 Income from the sale of merchandise, substantially all of which (at least 85%) was donated to the organization (section 513(a)(3)).

Specific Exceptions

06 Section 501 (c)(3), (4), or (5) organization conducting an agricultural or educational fair or exposition -Qualified public entertainment activity income (section 513(d)(2)).

07 Section 501 (c)(3), (4), (5), or (6) organization – Qualified convention and trade show activity income (section 513(d)(3)).

08 Income from hospital service described in section 513(e).

09 Income from noncommercial bingo games that do not violate state or local law (section 513(f)).

10 Income from games of chance conducted by an organization in North Dakota (section 311 of the Deficit Reduction Act of 1984, as amended).

11 Section 501(c)(l2) organization-Qualified pole rental income (section 513(g)).

12 Income from the distribution of low-cost articles in connection with the solicitation of charitable contributions (section 513(h)).

13 Income from the exchange or rental of membership or donor list with an organization eligible to receive charitable contributions by a (section 501(c)(3) organization; by a war veterans' organization; or an auxiliary unit or society of, or trust or foundation for, a war veterans' post or organization (section 513(h)).

Modifications and Exclusions

14 Dividends, interest, payments with respect to securities loans, annuities, income from notional principal contracts, loan commitment fees, and other substantially similar income from ordinary and routine investments excluded by (section 512(b)(1)).

15 Royalty income excluded by (section 512(b)(2)).

16 Real property rental income that does not depend on the income or profits derived by the person leasing the property and is excluded by (section 512 (b)(3)).

17 Rent from personal property leased with real property and incidental (10% or less) in relation to the combined income from the real and personal property (section 512(b)(3)).

18 Gain (or loss, to the extent allowed) from the sale of investments and other non-inventory property and from certain inventory property acquired from financial institutions that are in conservatorship or receivership (section 512(b)(5)).

19 Income or loss from the lapse or termination of options to buy or sell securities, or real property, and from the forfeiture of good-faith deposits for the purchase, sale, or lease of investment real property (section 512(b)(5)).

20 Income from research for the United States; its agencies or instrumentalities; or any state or political subdivision (section 512(b)7)).

21 Income from research conducted by a college, university, or hospital (section 512(b)(8)).

22 Income from research conducted by an organization whose primary activity is conducting fundamental research, the results of which are freely available to the general public (section 512(b)(9)).

23 Income from services provided under license issued by a Federal regulatory agency and conducted by a religious order or school operated by a religious order, but only if the trade or business has been carried on by the organization since before May 27. 1959 (section 512 (b)(l5)).

Foreign Organizations

24 Foreign organizations only – Income from a trade or business NOT conducted in the United States and NOT derived from United States sources (patrons) (section 512(a)(2)).

Social Clubs and VEBAs

25 Section 501(c)(7), (9), or (17) organization - Non-exempt function income set aside for a charitable, etc., purpose specified in (section 170(c)(4)) (section 512 (a)(3)(B)(l)).

26 Section 501(c)(7), (9), or (17) organization - Proceeds from the sale of exempt function property that was or will be timely reinvested in similar property (section 512(a)(3)(D)).

27 Section 501(c)(9). or (17) organization - Non-exempt function income set aside for the payment of life, sick, accident, or other benefits (section 512(a)(3)(B)(ii)).

Veterans' Organizations

28 Section 501(c)(19) organization-Payments for life, sick, accident, or health insurance for members or their dependents that are set aside for the payment of such insurance benefits or for a charitable, etc., purpose specified in (section 170(c)(4) (section 512(a)(4)).

29 Section 501 (c)(19) organization-Income from an insurance set-aside (see code 28 above) that is set aside for payment of insurance benefits or for a charitable, etc.. purpose specified in (section 170(c)(4). (Regulations section 1.512(a)-(4)(b)(2)).

Debt-financed Income

30 Income exempt from debt-financed (section 514) provisions because at least 85% of the use of the property is for the organization's exempt purposes (Note: This code is only for income from the 15% or less non-exempt purpose use.) (section 514(b)(1)(A)).

31 Gross income from mortgaged property used in research activities described in (section 512 (b)(7), (8) or (9)) (section 514(b)(1)(C)).

32 Gross income from mortgaged property used in any activity described in (section 513(a)(1), (2) or (3) (section 514(b)(1)(D)).

33 Income from mortgaged property (neighborhood land) acquired for exempt purpose use within 10 years (section 514(b)(3)).

34 Income from mortgaged property acquired by bequest or devise (applies to income received within 10 years from the date of acquisition) (section 514)(c)(2)(B)).

35 Income from mortgaged property acquired by gift where the mortgage was placed on the property more than 5 years previously and the property was held by the donor for more than 5 years (applies to income received within 10 years from the date of gift) (section 514(c)(2)(B)).

36 Income from property received in return for the obligation to pay an annuity described in section 514(c)(5).

37 Income from mortgaged property that provides housing to low and moderate income persons to the extent the mortgage is insured by the Federal Housing Administration (section 514(c)(6)) (Note: In many cases, this would be exempt function income reportable in column (E). It would not be so in the case of a (section 501 (c)(5) or (6) organization, for example, that acquired the housing as an investment or as a charitable activity.)

38 Income from mortgaged real property owned by: a school described in (section 170(b)(1)(A)(ii)); a (section 509(a)(3) affiliated support organization of such a school: a section 501 (c)(25) organization or by a partnership in which any of the above organizations owns an interest if the requirements of (section 514(c)(9)(B)(vi)) are met (section 514(c)(9)).

Special Rules

39 Section 501(c)(5) organization-Farm income used to finance the operation and maintenance of a retirement home, hospital, or similar facility operated by the organization for its members on property adjacent to the farm land (section 1951 (b)(8)(B) of Public Law 94-455).

Trade or Business

40 Gross income from an unrelated activity that is regularly carried on but, in light of continuous losses sustained over a number of tax periods, cannot be regarded as being conducted with the motive to make a profit (not a trade or business).

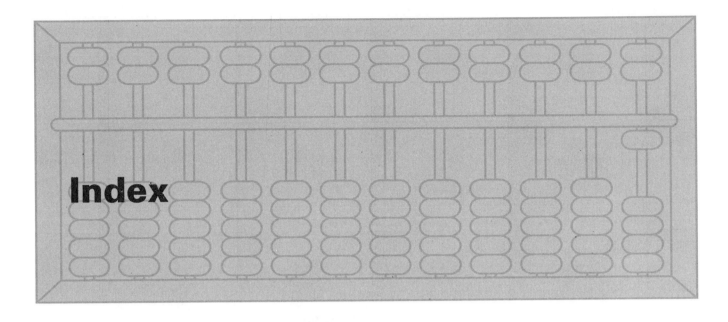

Index

A

S